The Official Presto® Pressure Cooker Cookbook

*Published by the makers of the
world famous Presto® Pressure Cooker:
National Presto Industries, Inc.
Eau Claire, Wisconsin*

ISBN 0-9654108-0-3
©1992, 1996, 1998 by National Presto Industries, Inc.
Part No. 59-659C

Contents

1. Introduction

Many modern food authorities consider the pressure cooker an absolutely essential part of a well-equipped kitchen. Surprised? You shouldn't be. Though a few folks may think of the pressure cooker as a relic, the truth is, its numerous advantages have never gone out of style. In fact, the pressure cooker has played an important role in the history and evolution of American food styles.

Pressure cooking saves time and energy by cooking foods three to ten times faster than ordinary methods. It's even faster than a microwave for many foods! Economical cuts of meat turn into delectably tender meals in minutes. Pressure cooking also preserves valuable nutrients, food flavors, and garden-fresh colors. Several foods, or even a whole meal, can be prepared at the same time in one pan. And, most importantly, foods cooked in the pressure cooker taste great.

Pressure cooking traces its roots back to the early nineteenth century when French confectioner Nicholas Appert, in an effort to better feed Napoleon's troops, made the first crude efforts at pressure canning. Over the next 100

1.

years, discoveries by scientists like Louis Pasteur helped the process to evolve and by the early 1900s pressure canning was perfected. In addition to its use in food preservation, the pressure canner also provided many benefits as a cooking device and was routinely doubling as a large capacity pressure cooker.

When the National Pressure Cooker Company (now National Presto Industries, Inc.) introduced the first saucepan-style home pressure cooker at the 1939 New York World's Fair, homemakers across the country called the Presto® pressure cooker a modern-day miracle. In addition to its compact size, this first *Presto® Cooker* featured an easy-to-close interlocking cover to seal the unit, eliminating the need for clumsy lug nuts and clamps.

So widespread was the consumers' acceptance of the *Presto® Cooker* that by the early forties pressure cooking was one of the most popular ways to prepare family meals.

The Depression was now over and money was more plentiful, but memories lingered and economy continued to be a major concern. The pressure cooker was an ideal way to get one's money's worth at the dinner table. Stores couldn't stock enough to meet demands. Every new bride counted on receiving a pressure cooker among her

The first Presto® Pressure Cooker introduced in 1939

gifts. It topped Mother's Day gift lists and found its way onto the pages of leading women's magazines, often with a recipe for one of the new food ideas coming out of Europe, like *Arroz con Pollo* (Chicken with Rice).

Then, in December 1941, Pearl Harbor was bombed. After only a few years of prosperity, Americans found themselves at war. Sacrificing, food rationing, and "making do" were once again commonplace. As women marched off to work in the defense plants, and meal preparation had to be simplified, the pressure cooker contributed to the war effort by becoming the homemaker's best ally in the fight against waste and inefficiency.

The war brought a temporary end to the manufacture of most aluminum cooking utensils, including pressure cookers. At the Presto factory in Wisconsin, facilities quickly converted to war work. Suddenly, just when consumers needed their pressure cookers most, there weren't enough to go around.

In a special footnote to a Presto advertisement in the July 1943 issue of *Life* magazine, the company encouraged homemakers to look forward to better times and to make pressure cooking part of their patriotic efforts:

The manufacturing facilities of the makers of PRESTO COOKERS are now devoted to war production. Once victory is won—there will be

PRESTO COOKERS for everybody. Until then, if you own one, share it, won't you? It's a good neighbor policy.

In 1945, with victory in sight, Presto resumed a portion of its civilian production. The pent-up demand for pressure cookers was tremendous. To assist homemakers who were eager to get their pressure cookers, Presto ran ads like the following one in *Woman's Home Companion*, dated October 1945:

To get your PRESTO Cooker sooner, See your dealer NOW.

PRESTO COOKERS are sold wherever quality housewares are available. Regular shipments of these wonderworking utensils are now being made. However, the tremendous demand for them exceeds the immediate supply. All requests are filled by dealers in the order in which they are received. So, see your dealer now, to get your PRESTO COOKER with the least possible delay.

In 1946, following that effective campaign, new ads were showing a smiling woman holding a new pressure cooker and exclaiming, "I'm so happy I waited for my PRESTO Cooker!" By the late forties the Presto® pressure cooker came in several sizes for a variety of home uses—from cooking for two to canning home grown fruits and vegetables.

With the decade drawing to a close, food was once again abundant and better than ever. Chocolate, coconut, pineapple, and bananas were back on the menu. Fancy new supermarkets replaced the little independent grocery stores and offered more services and specialty items. For the first time, consumers could buy chicken by the parts. Magazines tantalized readers with recipes for the exciting new foods the G.I.s brought back home

Intro

Basics

Appetizers

Soups and Stocks

Meats

Poultry

Seafood

Vegetables

Breads

Desserts

Whole Meal Magic

1.

from abroad. By the dawn of the fifties, pressure cookers were creating easier, faster, tastier meals in over 45 million American homes.

Certainly many of today's grown-up "baby boomers" can recall these familiar food memories from their childhood—Grandma making Sunday dinner pot roast in the pressure cooker or Mom pulling out the pressure cooker to put a weekday dinner on the table in a hurry.

But times were changing. As amazing advances in food technology continued to awe, pressure cookers were becoming overshadowed by a startling new discovery—convenience foods. Consumers were absolutely fascinated by the idea of "instant."

As early as 1951, supermarket shelves were overflowing with boxed mixes for batter and dough, bottled salad dressings and sauces, dry milk products, pie crust mixes, packaged soup mixes, and canned meats. First introduced in the forties, frozen foods, such as vegetables, fruits, meats, juices, and desserts became essential to quick and enjoyable meal preparation.

In 1953 the frozen dinner made its debut, dramatically changing America's eating habits and expectations. Suddenly quality and taste

took a back seat to convenience, as the country set off on a culinary course that made meals at the drive-in or in front of the TV more the norm than Mom's home cooking.

The relaxed expectations and easy-going lifestyles of the Eisenhower era did not last long. When 1960 rolled around, with it came an almost frantic urgency to try new things—to try everything.

Mass communications made the world smaller and exposed us to other cultures and cuisine. Travel broadened and ethnic cooking boomed. Exotic international ingredients found a new home in the stateside kitchens of self-proclaimed "gourmets." Hippies began preaching the benefits of health food, and "soul" food found new converts.

At trendy restaurants, nouvelle cuisine paired the unusual with the commonplace in intriguing, though somewhat minuscule, proportions. Meanwhile, home entertaining became a group activity, as everyone gathered around the fondue pot or the hibachi grill.

Over the next two decades this frenetic pace of experimentation slowed down and consumers settled into a new food sophistication. Having satisfied their curiosity, they began to appreciate simplicity and authenticity—pure, natural foods

"...real, hearty, home-cooked meals made fast and without a lot of fuss."

prepared by basic, less gimmicky cooking methods. Though the life-styles they chose were progressively more hectic and high-tech, ironically, they also felt a growing nostalgia for the past. So, they actively sought ways to make their homes more homey, their celebrations more traditional, and their foods more satisfying and comforting.

In this return to culinary roots, millions of pressure cookers were put back on the range. They were ideal for creating the kinds of food everyone suddenly craved: real, hearty, home-cooked meals made fast and without a lot of fuss.

Busy cooks discovered that no other cooking method or fancy kitchen gadget (including the microwave oven) was more efficient at

saving time, money, and energy. And no other method could create old-fashioned favorites with more authenticity or with more satisfying results.

Today, nutrition has become the latest national obsession. Nearly every day, newspaper headlines confirm the wisdom of sound nutrition based on the strong scientifically supported connection between diet and health.

Few consumers remain who are not conversant in the important elements of eating right: less fat, less cholesterol, and less sodium; more fiber, more complex carbohydrates, and more fresh or minimally processed foods. We now know that a varied diet based on whole grain breads and cereals, legumes, vegetables, fruits, low-fat dairy products, fish, skinless chicken, turkey, and lean meat is a necessity for good nutrition.

Unfortunately, many of us think cooking and eating for health is too difficult and too time consuming. We literally eat on the run, grabbing and gulping whatever is fast and easy. What we gain in time is lost in nutrition. When we rely heavily on commercially prepared foods, we're likely to get more of the things we don't need and less of the things we do.

That's why so many food authorities and nutritionists agree the best appliance you can have in your kitchen

Presto® Pressure Cooker introduced in 1998

Intro

Basics

Appetizers

Soups
and
Stocks

Meats

Poultry

Seafood

Vegetables

Breads

Desserts

Whole
Meal
Magic

> *"...pressure cooking is still the smart way to faster, healthier, tastier meals!"*

for convenience as well as nutritional benefits is the pressure cooker. When the pressure's on to eat right and eat well, you can't cook lighter, leaner, healthier, or faster than in the pressure cooker.

The fact that pressure cooking allows for fat-free food preparation is among its most noteworthy advantages. In issuing dietary guidelines, the federal government, American Dietetic Association, American Heart Association, American Cancer Society, National Research Council and a host of others all share some common concepts for good eating. Reducing fat, especially saturated fat, from the diet is the top priority for all of them.

With pressure cooking, liquid converted to steam, not fat, cooks the food. Using the cooking rack or basket inside the cooker also allows fats already in foods to drain down and out.

Shorter cooking times and the limited amount of water or liquid needed for cooking in the pressure cooker also rate high marks for helping boost the nutritional benefits of foods. With pressure cooking, all the important water-soluble vitamins, minerals, and flavor components are preserved in the preparation. And pressurized steam cooking literally enhances natural flavors so that

most food, even super-lean meats, taste savory and tempting without using lots of salt, sugar, and chemical additives.

Best of all, the speed and ease of pressure cooking can help even the most harried cook take advantage of the "fresh is best" philosophy of cooking. It's three to ten times faster than other cooking methods, yet it makes cooking savory, satisfying, healthy meals from scratch a pleasure!

All the delicious recipes developed by Presto for this special edition cookbook emphasize these important and timely advantages. They also reflect the evolution of American food tastes and current nutritional concerns. Recipes that are Low Calorie (300 calories or less) or Low Cholesterol (fewer than 80 milligrams of cholesterol per serving with 30% or less of the calories from fat) are conveniently identified. All recipes include nutrition information on calories, fat, sodium, and cholesterol per serving.

Perhaps in the next decade, every kitchen will be equipped with a pressure cooker and every cook will have discovered what you already know…that pressure cooking is still the smart way to faster, healthier, tastier meals!

2. Basics

You needn't be an experienced chef or a student of food science to master the art of pressure cooking. Simple principles and procedures are the secrets to its success at creating flavorful, tender, tempting foods in a mere fraction of the time. Armed with just a few basics, anyone can become "pressure cooker proficient" right from the start.

You don't have to be a rocket scientist to understand how pressure cooking works. When water (or any liquid) boils, it produces steam. A tightly sealed pressure cooker traps this steam, which then builds pressure inside the cooker. Under pressure, cooking temperatures rise significantly higher than possible under normal conditions. The super-heated steam created by these high temperatures cooks foods quickly, evenly, and deliciously. It also encourages an intense intermingling of flavors, when desired.

2.

No matter what brand or style, all pressure cookers work on the same principle. The following diagram illustrates the basic features of most newer pressure cookers. Of

tended to be a substitute for the manufacturer's instructions, which accompany your pressure cooker model, or for individual recipe instructions. They do, however, give

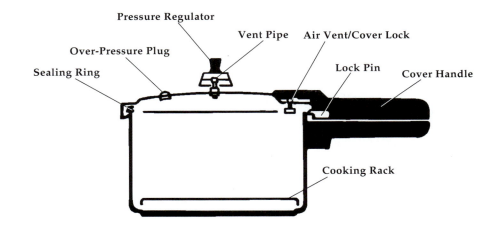

Pressure Regulator
Vent Pipe   Air Vent/Cover Lock
Over-Pressure Plug
Lock Pin   Cover Handle
Sealing Ring
Cooking Rack

course, you'll want to study your own model and get acquainted with exactly how it works.

Before you begin pressure cooking, take the time to read your pressure cooker instruction book and to practice assembling your pressure cooker properly. By doing this, you'll approach each new recipe with added confidence and learn how to properly clean and care for your pressure cooker to achieve perfect results every time.

It's also a good idea to have a basic understanding of the procedures involved. The following steps serve as a simple guide to using a pressure cooker. They are not in-

you a clear idea of just how simple it is to start pressure cooking.

1. Check the recipe in this book for specific instructions and the proper cooking time. Pour the required amount of liquid into the pressure cooker; then add food. Use a cooking rack or basket, if desired.

2. Hold the cover up to a light and look through the vent pipe to make certain it is open and unclogged. Then, place the cover on the pressure cooker and close it securely.

3. Place the pressure regulator firmly on the vent pipe. Heat the pressure cooker to 15 pounds pressure. Depending upon your model, 15 pounds pressure is reached when the pressure regulator begins to rock slowly or when a slow, steady release of steam is seen or heard. Adjust heat to maintain a slow, steady rocking motion or steam release. Cooking time begins at this point. When recipe states "cook 0 minutes," cook food only until 15 pounds pressure is reached.

4. Cook for the length of time specified in the recipe; then reduce pressure according to recipe directions. When recipe states "let pressure drop of its own accord," set the cooker aside to cool until the pressure is completely reduced. When recipe states "quick cool cooker," cool immediately under a cold water faucet until pressure is completely reduced or release quick cool dial according to manufacturer's instructions.

5. Pressure is completely reduced when the air vent/cover lock has dropped.

6. Remove cover and serve food.

Pressure Pointers

After more than half a century, pressure cooking has become predictable and virtually foolproof. If you follow the recipes and carefully monitor cooking times, the results should be perfect—and perfectly delicious—every time.

Here are some common questions people ask about pressure cooking:

Q **What liquids can I use in the pressure cooker?**

A Many different cooking liquids can be used in the pressure cooker. Water is the liquid used most often, but an abundance of rich sauces and gravies can result from the use of bouillon or stock, wine, beer, and even fruit and vegetable juices. You're only limited by your imagination!

Q **How much liquid should I use for pressure cooking?**

A You must have liquid to create steam, so it follows that you must always use some form of cooking liquid in the pressure cooker. Since there is very little evaporation from a sealed pressure cooker, it isn't necessary to use a great deal of cooking liquid.

Q **How much food fits safely in a pressure cooker?**

A Pressure cookers of different sizes have different food capacities. *Read your instruction booklet carefully to determine what is correct for your pressure cooker.* Generally, the food should not come up so high in the pressure cooker that there is a possibility it will block the vent pipe or overpressure plug. That is why

2.

most manufacturers recommend that the pressure cooker not be filled more than two-thirds full. In addition, certain foods tend to expand at a greater rate during cooking. For these foods, recipes will caution you not to fill the pressure cooker more than one-half full. The recipes in this cookbook were tested in a 6-quart pressure cooker. If your pressure cooker is smaller, check your manual to make sure the recipe does not exceed the recommended limit of your model.

Q How is cooking time measured in pressure cooking?

A Foods cook quickly in the pressure cooker, so precise timing is important to avoid overcooking. *Pressure cooking time is measured from the point at which the correct level of pressure is reached. Always use a timer.* The time it takes for the food to reach 15 pounds pressure depends upon how much and what kind of food is in the pressure cooker. It will vary with each recipe. Always use high heat to bring the pressure cooker up to pressure. Then reduce the heat to maintain a steady level. When the specified cooking time is complete, reduce pressure in the cooker

according to the directions in the recipe.

Q How is pressure reduced in the pressure cooker?

A When cooking is complete there are several ways to reduce pressure within the pressure cooker. Which method you use usually depends upon the type of food you are cooking. The recipe will specify which method to use. Quick cooling is usually used for delicate foods such as custards and fresh vegetables. Because there are various quick cooling procedures, refer to the instruction booklet that accompanies your pressure cooker. For denser foods, like roasts or stews, it is usually recommended that you let the pressure cooker cool of its own accord by setting it aside until the pressure drops completely. This can take anywhere from 2 to 20 minutes depending on what you are cooking.

Q Does altitude affect pressure cooking?

A Yes, because altitude affects the point at which water boils. When pressure cooking at high altitudes, the cooking time should be increased 5% for every

1000 feet above 2000 feet. Increase cooking time as follows:

3000 feet — 5%
4000 feet — 10%
5000 feet — 15%
6000 feet — 20%
7000 feet — 25%
8000 feet — 30%

Q When should the cooking rack or basket be used?

A The cooking rack or basket are used when it is desirable to keep some or all of the food out of the cooking liquid. This is especially important when cooking several types of food or an entire meal in the pressure cooker at one time. Foods kept out of the cooking liquid maintain the purity of their own distinct flavors and aromas. When you want flavors to intermingle, don't use the cooking rack or basket.

Q What kinds of utensils can be used inside a pressure cooker?

A Ovenproof glass, metal, and ceramic dishes—from soufflé dishes to ramekins, custard cups, and spring form pans—can be used in the pressure cooker for beautifully displayed desserts and side dishes. Fill dishes two-thirds full to allow for expansion of foods and fit them loosely into the pressure cooker on the cooking rack or in the basket.

Pressure cooking is simplicity itself once you know the basics. Now it's time to try your hand at creating fast, healthy, tasty meals in *your* pressure cooker using these specially developed recipes.

● ● ● ● ● ● ●

Intro

Basics

Appetizers

Soups
and
Stocks

Meats

Poultry

Seafood

Vegetables

Breads

Desserts

Whole
Meal
Magic

15

Notes

3. Appetizers

Over the last 60 years, appetizers have occupied a variety of positions on the American food scene. During the frugal forties, few meals in this country featured first courses. When the soldiers returned after the war, celebrations returned as well and appetizers appeared with a vengeance! Cheese balls, deviled eggs, bacon-crab rolls, and dozens of dips, made for the first time with commercially prepared sour cream, kept us festive right on into the fifties.

Even Ike's heart attack and the first warnings about fat and cholesterol did little to dampen the American spirit of celebration. Rich, calorie-laden canapés continued to find favor at cocktail parties, dinner parties, and even casual get-togethers.

Exotic, ethnic, and natural foods entered the appetizer arena in the experimental sixties. Traditional sit-down meals with separate courses faded with the arrival of the fondue pot and the smorgasbord. By the eighties, appetizers had actually become the meal! "Grazing" was the latest trend, with everyone eating several appetizer-size portions of many different foods.

3.

Our fascination with first courses continues today. We now have decades of appetizer ideas from which to choose, and our choices are becoming more sophisticated and savvy. Whether we opt for elegance or a casual effect, we look for ways to cut calories, fat, and cholesterol without sacrificing style or taste. We also rely heavily on cooking methods and recipes that help us save time and effort.

The pressure cooker, though not usually associated with appetizer cookery, is surprisingly adept at creating fast, flavorful first courses. In this chapter, you'll find a wide array of appetizer recipes that cook to perfection in the pressure cooker and get you off to a fast start—from fancy company pleasers like *Seafood Mousse* to popular family fare, such as *Oriental Ribs* and *Chicken Drumettes Teriyaki*. We've even included a historical nod to our country's unique regional food heritage with *Southern-Style Boiled Peanuts*.

● ● ● ● ● ● ●

❋ *Low Calorie*
Servings: 16
Per Serving
Calories: 112
Fat: 8.7 g
Sodium: 532 mg
Cholesterol: 18 mg

Chicken Drumettes Teriyaki

3 **pounds chicken wings**
1 **cup soy sauce**
½ **cup vegetable oil**
½ **cup dry sherry or white wine**

2 **teaspoons grated orange rind**
2 **cloves garlic, minced**
½ **teaspoon ground ginger**

Cut meaty "drumette" section from chicken wings. Reserve remaining wing sections for another use. Combine drumettes with remaining ingredients in plastic bag or glass dish. Close bag securely or cover dish. Marinate in refrigerator overnight. Place cooking rack (or basket) and marinade in pressure cooker. Place drumettes on rack (or in basket). Close cover securely. Place pressure regulator on vent pipe. COOK 4 MINUTES at 15 pounds pressure. Let pressure drop of its own accord.

Sausage-Stuffed Cheese

1 (7- or 8-ounce) Gouda, Cheddar or Monterey Jack cheese
½ pound hot seasoned pork sausage
1 clove garlic, minced
1 tablespoon tomato paste
1 teaspoon chili powder
½ teaspoon dried oregano
½ teaspoon ground coriander
1½ cups water

* * * * *

Tortilla chips

❀ Low Calorie
Servings: 8
Per Serving
Calories: 174
Fat: 13.9 g
Sodium: 512 mg
Cholesterol: 47 mg

Remove wax coating from cheese, if coated. Cut Gouda horizontally in half, or cut a 1½-inch slice of Cheddar or Monterey Jack cheese to fit a 2-cup casserole. Place half of cheese in the 2-cup casserole. Shred remaining cheese. Crumble sausage and cook with garlic in skillet over medium heat until brown. Discard excess fat. Mix tomato paste, chili powder, oregano, and coriander with sausage. Spoon sausage mixture over cheese in casserole. Top with shredded cheese. Cover casserole securely with aluminum foil. Place cooking rack (or basket) and water in pressure cooker. Place casserole on rack (or in basket). Close cover securely. Place pressure regulator on vent pipe. COOK 5 MINUTES at 15 pounds pressure. Quick cool cooker. Serve immediately with tortilla chips.

● ● ● ● ● ● ●

Shrimp Mariniere

1½ cups dry white wine
4 shallots or 1 onion, chopped
½ teaspoon salt
¼ teaspoon pepper
Bouquet garni (thyme, bay leaf, parsley, tied in cheesecloth)
2 pounds medium shrimp in shells

* * * * *

3 tablespoons chopped parsley
Crusty bread

❀ Low Calorie
Servings: 8
Per Serving
Calories: 120
Fat: 1 g
Sodium: 336 mg
Cholesterol: 174 mg

Combine wine, shallots, salt, pepper, and bouquet garni in pressure cooker. Place cooking rack (or basket) in pressure cooker. Place shrimp on rack (or in basket). Close cover securely. Place pressure regulator on vent pipe. COOK 1 MINUTE at 15 pounds pressure. Quick cool cooker. Discard bouquet garni. Ladle shrimp and cooking liquid into bowls. Sprinkle with parsley. Serve with crusty bread.

Intro
Basics
Appetizers
Soups and Stocks
Meats
Poultry
Seafood
Vegetables
Breads
Desserts
Whole Meal Magic

Poached Garlic Heads

4 small heads garlic	1½ cups water
8 teaspoons margarine	* * * * *
¼ teaspoon dried thyme	French bread, sliced
⅛ teaspoon salt	

❋ Low Calorie
Servings: 4
Per Serving
Calories: 68
Fat: 7.6 g
Sodium: 155 mg
Cholesterol: 0

Carefully cut tops off garlic cloves on each head. Wrap a 4-inch piece of aluminum foil loosely around bottom of each garlic head. Dot garlic with margarine. Sprinkle with thyme and salt. Place cooking rack (or basket) and water in pressure cooker. Place garlic on rack (or in basket). Close cover securely. Place pressure regulator on vent pipe. COOK 10 MINUTES at 15 pounds pressure. Let pressure drop of its own accord. Remove garlic. Pour margarine mixture from foil over each head. To eat, spread garlic on bread.

Seafood Mousse

❋ Low Calorie
Servings: 8
Per Serving
Calories: 186
Fat: 16 g
Sodium: 361 mg
Cholesterol: 50 mg

8 ounces skinless fish fillets (cod, whitefish, orange roughy, or salmon)	Dash red pepper sauce
	2 ounces bay scallops or coarsely chopped sea scallops
2 egg whites	2 ounces shrimp, shelled, deveined, coarsely chopped
½ cup whipping cream	2 cups water
1 tablespoon tomato paste	* * * * *
1 tablespoon dry sherry, optional	½ cup mayonnaise
2 teaspoons dried tarragon	1 tablespoon lemon juice
¾ teaspoon salt	1 teaspoon chopped chives

Cut fish into 1-inch pieces; process in food processor until smooth. With motor running, add egg whites; add cream slowly. Stop motor. Add tomato paste, sherry, tarragon, salt, and pepper sauce. Process until well mixed. Stir in scallops and shrimp. Pack mixture into greased ovenproof glass or foil loaf pan, 6 x 3 x 2 inches. Cover pan securely with aluminum foil. Place cooking rack (or basket) and water in pressure cooker. Place pan on rack (or in basket). Close cover securely. Place pressure regulator on vent pipe. COOK 15 MINUTES at 15 pounds pressure. Let pressure drop of its own accord. Mousse should feel firm to touch and will shrink from sides of pan slightly. Remove mousse and refrigerate until chilled. To serve, unmold mousse and cut into slices. Mix mayonnaise, lemon juice, and chives. Serve with mousse.

Red Lentil-Yogurt Dip

¾ cup dried red lentils
2 tablespoons vegetable oil
1½ teaspoons salt
Cold water to cover lentils
1 tablespoon olive oil
½ cup chopped onion
1 large clove garlic, minced

¼ teaspoon ground nutmeg
1¾ cups chicken stock or broth

* * * * *

3-4 tablespoons plain yogurt
Salt
Pita bread, cut into triangles
Fresh vegetable relishes

❀ *Low Calorie*
Servings: 12
Per Serving
Calories: 69
Fat: 3.7 g
Sodium: 383 mg
Cholesterol: 0

Soak lentils overnight in vegetable oil, salt, and cold water to cover; drain. Heat olive oil in pressure cooker over medium heat. Sauté onion, garlic, and nutmeg until onion is tender. Stir in chicken stock and lentils. Close cover securely. Place pressure regulator on vent pipe. COOK 7 MINUTES at 15 pounds pressure. Let pressure drop of its own accord. Process lentil mixture in food processor or blender until smooth. Stir in yogurt. Season to taste with salt. Refrigerate until chilled. Serve with pita bread and vegetables for dipping.

● ● ● ● ● ● ●

Chinese-Style Mushroom Caps

18 large mushroom caps
(about ¾ pound)
½ pound ground extra lean pork
2 green onions, finely chopped
2 tablespoons rice wine or
sherry
2 tablespoons cornstarch

1 tablespoon soy sauce
1 tablespoon sesame oil
2 teaspoons sugar
1 clove garlic, minced
1½ cups water

* * * * *

Hot mustard

❀ *Low Calorie*
Servings: 18
Per Serving
Calories: 35
Fat: 1.3 g
Sodium: 64 mg
Cholesterol: 9 mg

Remove stems from mushrooms. Finely chop stems. Combine chopped stems, pork, green onions, rice wine, cornstarch, soy sauce, sesame oil, sugar, and garlic. Stuff mushroom caps with mixture. Place cooking rack (or basket) and water in pressure cooker. Place single layer of mushrooms on rack (or in basket). Close cover securely. Place pressure regulator on vent pipe. COOK 5 MINUTES at 15 pounds pressure. Quick cool cooker. Repeat above procedure to cook remaining mushrooms. Serve mushrooms with hot mustard.

Intro

Basics

Appetizers

Soups
and
Stocks

Meats

Poultry

Seafood

Vegetables

Breads

Desserts

Whole
Meal
Magic

21

Shrimp-Stuffed Artichokes

4 medium artichokes	¾ cup fresh bread crumbs
2 tablespoons margarine	½ cup chopped shelled deveined shrimp
1 tablespoon finely chopped green pepper	¼ cup shredded Swiss cheese
1 tablespoon finely chopped onion	1 egg white
1 small clove garlic, minced	1½ cups water

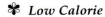 **Low Calorie**

Servings: 4
Per Serving
Calories: 201
Fat: 8.4 g
Sodium: 315 mg
Cholesterol: 28 mg

(Shown on page 51)

Cut 1½ inches off top of each artichoke. Cut off stems. Pull leaves open at top, remove center leaves and scrape out choke with grapefruit spoon. Heat margarine in small skillet over medium heat. Sauté green pepper, onion, and garlic until tender. Remove from heat. Stir in bread crumbs, shrimp, cheese, and egg white. Spoon filling into centers of artichokes. Place cooking rack (or basket) and water in pressure cooker. Place artichokes on rack (or in basket). Close cover securely. Place pressure regulator on vent pipe. COOK 8 MINUTES at 15 pounds pressure. Quick cool cooker. Pull several leaves from bottoms of artichokes and check doneness. If necessary, repeat above procedure, cooking for 1 or 2 minutes. Serve warm.

● ● ● ● ● ● ●

Low Calorie
Low Cholesterol
Servings: 8
Per Serving
Calories: 112
Fat: 0
Sodium: 5 mg
Cholesterol: 0

Glögg

1 cinnamon stick	✴ ✴ ✴ ✴ ✴
4 whole cloves	1 (25½-ounce) bottle red burgundy wine
1½ cups water	½ cup sugar
½ orange, cut into quarters	
½ lemon, cut into quarters	

Tie spices in small piece of cheesecloth. Combine water, orange, lemon, and spices in pressure cooker. Close cover securely. Place pressure regulator on vent pipe. COOK 5 MINUTES at 15 pounds pressure. Let pressure drop of its own accord. Stir in wine and sugar. Simmer uncovered for 5 to 10 minutes. Discard spices and fruit. Serve warm.

Three-Cheese Cheesecake

Margarine
Dry unseasoned bread crumbs
1 (8-ounce) package cream cheese, softened
½ cup crumbled blue cheese
¼ cup shredded Monterey Jack cheese
⅓ cup sour cream or sour half-and-half
2 eggs
¼ cup mild or medium chunky salsa

2 tablespoons all-purpose flour
1 clove garlic, minced
⅛ teaspoon ground cumin
3 cups water

* * * * *

Chives or green onions, thinly sliced
French bread, thinly sliced, toasted, or crackers

❋ Low Calorie
Servings: 12
Per Serving
Calories: 125
Fat: 11 g
Sodium: 167 mg
Cholesterol: 65 mg

Line 1-quart soufflé dish that fits loosely on rack (or in basket) in pressure cooker with aluminum foil; coat generously with margarine, then with bread crumbs. Beat cheeses and sour cream in small bowl until fluffy. Beat in eggs and salsa. Beat in flour, garlic, and cumin. Pour into soufflé dish. Cover dish securely with foil. Place cooking rack (or basket) and water in cooker. Place soufflé dish on rack (or in basket). Close cover securely. Place pressure regulator on vent pipe. COOK 40 MINUTES at 15 pounds pressure. Quick cool cooker. Remove cheesecake and refrigerate 8 hours or overnight. Remove cheesecake from dish by lifting foil. Carefully remove foil. Sprinkle with chives. Serve with bread or crackers.

• • • • • • •

Hot Spiced Cider

1 quart apple cider
1 cinnamon stick, broken into halves

3 whole cardamom pods
3 whole cloves

❋ Low Calorie
♥ Low Cholesterol
Servings: 4
Per Serving
Calories: 94
Fat: 0
Sodium: 0
Cholesterol: 0

Combine cider and spices in pressure cooker. Close cover securely. Place pressure regulator on vent pipe. COOK 5 MINUTES at 15 pounds pressure. Let pressure drop of its own accord. Discard spices. Serve cider warm.

Intro

Basics

Appetizers

Soups and Stocks

Meats

Poultry

Seafood

Vegetables

Breads

Desserts

Whole Meal Magic

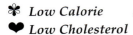

3.

Citrus Scallops

1 cup dry white wine	2 teaspoons cornstarch
8 ounces sea scallops	1 teaspoon margarine
1 tablespoon grated lemon rind	¼ teaspoon sugar
1 tablespoon grated orange rind	Salt
* * * * *	Toasted sesame seeds
1 tablespoon orange-flavored liqueur	

❀ *Low Calorie*
❤ *Low Cholesterol*

Servings: 4
Per Serving
Calories: 80
Fat: 1.5 g
Sodium: 44 mg
Cholesterol: 19 mg

Place rack (or basket) and wine in pressure cooker. Place scallops on rack (or in basket). Sprinkle scallops with 1 teaspoon each of the lemon and orange rinds. Close cover securely. Place pressure regulator on vent pipe. COOK 1 MINUTE at 15 pounds pressure. Quick cool cooker. Remove scallops and keep warm. Remove rack (or basket). Mix liqueur and cornstarch. Stir into wine in pressure cooker. Cook and stir until sauce boils and thickens. Stir in margarine, sugar, and remaining 2 teaspoons each lemon and orange rinds. Season to taste with salt. Spoon sauce over scallops. Sprinkle with sesame seeds.

● ● ● ● ● ● ●

❀ *Low Calorie*
Servings: 8
Per Serving
Calories: 166
Fat: 12.9 g
Sodium: 261 mg
Cholesterol: 8 mg

Walnut-Sherry Mushroom Caps

24 large mushrooms	3 egg whites
¼ cup margarine	3 tablespoons dry sherry or chicken stock or broth
¼ cup finely chopped onion	
⅔ cup shredded Swiss cheese	1 teaspoon packed brown sugar
½ cup fresh bread crumbs	½ teaspoon salt
½ cup finely chopped walnuts	1½ cups water

Remove stems from mushrooms. Chop stems finely. Heat margarine in skillet over medium heat. Sauté mushroom stems and onion until tender. Remove from heat. Stir in cheese, bread crumbs, walnuts, egg whites, sherry, sugar, and salt. Stuff mushroom caps with mixture. Place cooking rack (or basket) and water in pressure cooker. Place half the mushrooms on rack (or in basket). Close cover securely. Place pressure regulator on vent pipe. COOK 2 MINUTES at 15 pounds pressure. Quick cool cooker. Remove mushrooms and keep warm. Repeat above procedure to cook remaining mushrooms.

Duck Rillettes

2½ cups water
1 (3½- to 4-pound) duckling,
  cut into 2-inch pieces
  * * * * *
1 tablespoon brandy or
  Cognac, optional

2 bay leaves
  French bread
  Cornichons or small sweet
  gherkins

✿ Low Calorie
Servings: 12
Per Serving
Calories: 196
Fat: 16.3 g
Sodium: 34 mg
Cholesterol: 48 mg

Place cooking rack (or basket) and water in pressure cooker. Place duck on rack (or in basket). Close cover securely. Place pressure regulator on vent pipe. COOK 40 MINUTES at 15 pounds pressure. Quick cool cooker. Remove duck and cool. Refrigerate pan juices until fat solidifies on top. Remove duck meat from bones. Discard skin and bones. Shred duck meat with fork. Combine duck with brandy, 3 tablespoons duck fat, and ½ cup pan juices and mix gently. Place bay leaves in bottoms of two 8-ounce custard cups. Pack duck mixture into cups. Refrigerate until serving time. Unmold and serve with bread and cornichons.

● ● ● ● ● ● ●

Chicken Satay

8 ounces boneless skinless
  chicken breast
¼ cup honey
2 tablespoons light soy sauce
1½ cups water
  * * * * *
½ cup smooth peanut butter
¼ cup light soy sauce
3 tablespoons sesame oil

2 tablespoons red wine
  vinegar
1 tablespoon ground ginger
1 tablespoon minced garlic
1 tablespoon packed brown
  sugar
1-2 teaspoons Szechwan chili
  sauce
  Warm water

✿ Low Calorie
Servings: 6
Per Serving
Calories: 279
Fat: 18 g
Sodium: 684 mg
Cholesterol: 15 mg

Cut 12 wooden skewers into 4-inch lengths. Cut chicken into 12 long strips and thread onto skewers. Mix honey and 2 tablespoons soy sauce. Brush on chicken; let stand 5 minutes. Place cooking rack (or basket) and water in pressure cooker. Place skewers on rack (or in basket). Close cover securely. Place pressure regulator on vent pipe. COOK 2 MINUTES at 15 pounds pressure. Quick cool cooker. Mix remaining ingredients, adding enough warm water to make dipping consistency. Serve with warm chicken.

Intro

Basics

Appetizers

Soups
and
Stocks

Meats

Poultry

Seafood

Vegetables

Breads

Desserts

Whole
Meal
Magic

Southern-Style Boiled Peanuts

6 cups water
⅓ cup salt
1 pound raw peanuts in the shell*

❉ *Low Calorie*
Servings: 16
Per Serving
Calories: 90
Fat: 6.2 g
Sodium: 213 mg
Cholesterol: 0

Place water in 6- or 8-quart pressure cooker. Stir in salt. Add peanuts. Close cover securely. Place pressure regulator on vent pipe. COOK 40 MINUTES at 15 pounds pressure. Let pressure drop of its own accord. Let peanuts cool in cooking water, then drain.

*Raw peanuts in the shell can be purchased in health food stores and in many supermarkets.

● ● ● ● ● ● ●

❉ *Low Calorie*
Servings: 16
Per Serving
Calories: 24
Fat: 1.8 g
Sodium: 3 mg
Cholesterol: 0

Eggplant Dip

1½ cups water
1 medium eggplant (about 1 pound), cut into halves
✳ ✳ ✳ ✳ ✳
2 tablespoons tahini (sesame seed paste)*
1 tablespoon olive or vegetable oil
3 cloves garlic

1 teaspoon dried sage
¼-½ teaspoon red pepper sauce
2-3 tablespoons lemon juice
Salt
Pepper
Parsley, minced
Pita bread, cut into triangles or cracker bread

Place cooking rack (or basket) and water in pressure cooker. Place eggplant, cut sides up, on rack (or in basket). Close cover securely. Place pressure regulator on vent pipe. COOK 5 MINUTES at 15 pounds pressure. Quick cool cooker. Eggplant should be very tender; if necessary, repeat above procedure, cooking 1 or 2 minutes. When eggplant is cool enough to handle, remove skin. Coarsely chop eggplant. Process eggplant, tahini, oil, garlic, sage, and pepper sauce in food processor or blender until smooth. Season to taste with lemon juice, salt, and pepper. Spoon into bowl. Sprinkle with parsley. Serve with pita bread.

*Tahini can be purchased in Greek grocery stores or in the specialty department of many supermarkets. Two tablespoons toasted crushed sesame seeds can be substituted.

Anise Tea

1 quart water
2 orange pekoe tea bags
3 star anise

Combine water, tea bags, and star anise in pressure cooker. Close cover securely. Place pressure regulator on vent pipe. COOK 30 SECONDS at 15 pounds pressure. Let pressure drop of its own accord. Discard star anise and tea bags.

♣ *Low Calorie*
♥ *Low Cholesterol*
Servings: 6
Per Serving
Calories: 2
Fat: 0
Sodium: 5 mg
Cholesterol: 0

● ● ● ● ● ● ●

Peppercorn Terrine

1 tablespoon margarine or
  vegetable oil
⅓ cup finely chopped onion
¼ cup finely chopped
  mushrooms
1 clove garlic, minced
1 pound ground turkey or
  chicken
½ pound ground veal
⅓ cup fresh French bread
  crumbs

1 egg
1-2 tablespoons brandy or
  Cognac, optional
1 tablespoon green
  peppercorns in brine,
  drained
½ teaspoon dried rosemary
2½ cups water

＊ ＊ ＊ ＊ ＊

French bread
Dijon-style mustard

♣ *Low Calorie*
Servings: 10
Per Serving
Calories: 100
Fat: 5.3 g
Sodium: 59 mg
Cholesterol: 52 mg

Heat margarine in cooker over medium heat. Sauté onion, mushrooms, and garlic until tender. Mix turkey, veal, bread crumbs, egg, brandy, peppercorns, rosemary, and sautéed vegetables. Pack mixture firmly into 2 metal or foil loaf pans, 6 x 3 x 2 inches. Place cooking rack (or basket) and water in pressure cooker. Place pans on rack (or in basket). Close cover securely. Place pressure regulator on vent pipe. COOK 25 MINUTES at 15 pounds pressure. Let pressure drop of its own accord. Remove terrines, cover with aluminum foil, and refrigerate overnight, weighted with l-pound cans. Remove terrines from pans. Cut into thin slices. Serve with French bread and mustard.

Intro

Basics

Appetizers

Soups
and
Stocks

Meats

Poultry

Seafood

Vegetables

Breads

Desserts

Whole
Meal
Magic

27

3.

Oriental Ribs

½ cup catsup
2 tablespoons honey
2 teaspoons teriyaki sauce
½ teaspoon garlic powder
½ teaspoon ground allspice
½ teaspoon pepper

1 pound boneless country ribs, cut into 1½ -inch pieces
2 cups beer

* * * * *

Salt

❋ *Low Calorie*
Servings: 8
Per Serving
Calories: 100
Fat: 5.2 g
Sodium: 212 mg
Cholesterol: 11 mg

Mix catsup, honey, teriyaki sauce, garlic powder, allspice, and pepper. Pour over ribs in glass bowl. Marinate 30 minutes. Place cooking rack (or basket) and beer in pressure cooker. Remove ribs from marinade and place on rack (or in basket), reserving marinade. Close cover securely. Place pressure regulator on vent pipe. COOK 15 MINUTES at 15 pounds pressure. Quick cool cooker. Remove ribs and rack (or basket); keep warm. Add reserved marinade to pressure cooker. Boil, stirring constantly, until mixture is reduced to ½ cup, about 5 minutes. Season to taste with salt. Spoon over ribs.

● ● ● ● ● ●

❋ *Low Calorie*
Servings: 12
Per Serving
Calories: 52
Fat: 3.9 g
Sodium: 38 mg
Cholesterol: 3 mg

(Shown on page 51)

Vegetables with Curried Dill Dip

1 pound brussels sprouts, trimmed*
1 cup water

* * * * *

¼ cup mayonnaise

¼ cup plain yogurt
1 tablespoon lemon juice
1 teaspoon dillweed
½ teaspoon curry powder
¼ teaspoon sugar

If brussels sprouts are large, cut an "x" in the stem ends. Place cooking rack (or basket) and water in pressure cooker. Place brussels sprouts on rack (or in basket). Close cover securely. Place pressure regulator on vent pipe. COOK 1½ TO 2 MINUTES at 15 pounds pressure. Quick cool cooker. Rinse sprouts under cold water. Refrigerate until chilled. Cut sprouts into halves. Combine remaining ingredients. Serve as a dipping sauce with sprouts.

*Pick your choice of other vegetables to serve, such as cauliflower, carrots, beets, etc. Use minimum cooking times suggested for basic pressure cooking of vegetables.

Steamed Pork and Shrimp Dumplings

✽ *Low Calorie*
♥ *Low Cholesterol*
Servings: 36
Per Serving
Calories: 32
Fat: 0.5 g
Sodium: 42 mg
Cholesterol: 13 mg

1 large dried Chinese black mushroom
  Hot water
4 ounces ground lean pork
4 ounces shrimp, shelled, deveined, finely chopped
2 tablespoons finely chopped water chestnuts
2 small green onions (white parts only), minced

2 teaspoons soy sauce
1 teaspoon dry sherry, optional
1 teaspoon sesame oil
1 teaspoon cornstarch
½ teaspoon sugar
¼ teaspoon salt
  Pinch pepper
36 round wonton wrappers (3½-inch)*
1½ cups water

Soak mushroom in hot water until softened, about 20 minutes. Drain and finely chop, discarding stem and tough center. Mix mushroom, pork, shrimp, water chestnuts, green onions, soy sauce, sherry, sesame oil, cornstarch, sugar, salt, and pepper. Place generous teaspoon of the mixture in center of each wonton wrapper. Bring sides of wrappers up around filling, pinching around filling to form bundles. Lightly press down on filling. Place cooking rack (or basket) and water in pressure cooker. Place half the dumplings on rack (or in basket). Close cover securely. Place pressure regulator on vent pipe. COOK 5 MINUTES at 15 pounds pressure. Quick cool cooker. Remove dumplings and keep warm. Repeat above procedure to cook remaining dumplings. Serve with Sesame-Soy Dipping Sauce.

* Wonton wrappers can be purchased in Oriental grocery stores and in many supermarkets. Square wonton or egg roll wrapper can be used; cut into rounds with 3½-inch cutter.

Sesame-Soy Dipping Sauce

✽ *Low Calorie*
Servings: 36
Per Serving
Calories: 10
Fat: 0.7 g
Sodium: 152 mg
Cholesterol: 0

⅓ cup soy sauce
2 tablespoons sesame oil

2 tablespoons dry sherry
1½ teaspoons sugar

Mix soy sauce, sesame oil, dry sherry, and sugar in bowl. Makes about ½ cup.

Intro

Basics

Appetizers

Soups
and
Stocks

Meats

Poultry

Seafood

Vegetables

Breads

Desserts

Whole
Meal
Magic

Notes

4. Soups and Stocks

Though most of us think of soup-making as hard, time-consuming work, homemade soups may have been the original "convenience" foods! In the days of hearth-side cooking, American homemakers always kept a pot of water on the back of the fire. Leftover meat and vegetables would be thrown into the pot and left to simmer all day. On busy days, when the chores left no time to cook a proper meal, there was always plenty of hot soup to go around.

It's only logical then that Campbell's canned condensed soup, introduced in the late 1890s, quickly captured the hearts of convenience craving consumers. By the 1950s, this shortcut to soup had become a standard in nearly every American kitchen. It was great for quick lunches, weekday suppers, after school snacks, and to jazz up casseroles. No serious hostess, however, would serve it to company!

Instead, she might turn to the pages of *Better Homes and Gardens* magazine to find a recipe for an impressive homemade soup. Perhaps she would try "Pottage Elegante," a caloric and cholesterol-heavy concoction prepared with browned beef bones, puréed vegetables, egg yolks, heavy cream, and then topped with grated Parmesan cheese.

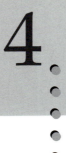

4.

"Cool" sixties' gourmets made vichyssoise a household word, while the seventies saw seafood chowders, like bouillabaisse and cioppino, become popular. In the late eighties, aging baby boomers made homemade soup their ultimate "comfort" food—a nostalgic symbol of home, hearth, family, and nurturing. Unfortunately, this craving for savory, long-simmered soups of the past clashed with a new, even more desperate dependence on convenience and quick fixes.

Luckily, the pressure cooker really brings soup-making up to speed! Hearty, satisfying, made-from-scratch soups that would take hours of simmering in a conventional pot require mere minutes in the pressure cooker. And speed is only one of the advantages.

Soups actually come out of the pressure cooker with a richer, more full-bodied taste. The pressurized steam intensifies and enhances natural flavors like no length of stove top simmering ever could.

This chapter provides a range of pressure cooker soup recipes that reflect current tastes as well as America's "melting pot"—the delicious diversity of its history, regions, and cultural influences. Among these are *Black Bean Soup* from the Caribbean, *Mexican Chicken & Corn Soup,* and *Mulligatawny* from India. You'll also discover recipes for the quickest, easiest, richest stocks you've ever prepared at home.

Minestrone

1 tablespoon vegetable oil
1½ pounds lean boneless beef,
   cut into 1-inch cubes
6 cups water
2 carrots, sliced
1 onion, diced
¼ cup chopped celery
2 tablespoons parsley flakes
2 teaspoons salt
1½ teaspoons dried basil
1 clove garlic, minced
¼ teaspoon pepper

1 bay leaf
* * * * *
1 (16-ounce) can cut green
   beans, drained
1 (15-ounce) jar great northern
   beans, drained, rinsed
1 (8-ounce) can tomatoes,
   undrained, coarsely chopped
4 ounces Polish sausage,
   thinly sliced
2 ounces fine noodles
   Grated Parmesan cheese

Servings: 8
Per Serving
Calories: 304
Fat: 12.2 g
Sodium: 872 mg
Cholesterol: 74 mg

(Shown on page 58)

Heat oil in 6- or 8-quart pressure cooker over medium heat. Brown beef. Stir in water, carrots, onion, celery, parsley flakes, salt, basil, garlic, pepper, and bay leaf. Close cover securely. Place pressure regulator on vent pipe. COOK 15 MINUTES at 15 pounds pressure. Let pressure drop of its own accord. Add green beans, great northern beans, tomatoes, sausage, and noodles. Simmer, uncovered, for 10 minutes. Serve with cheese.

● ● ● ● ● ● ●

Peasant Garlic Soup

2 cups water
1½ cups diced pared potatoes
1 cup chopped carrot
1 cup sliced celery
1 cup chicken stock or broth
2 heads garlic, peeled
1 teaspoon dried thyme

1 teaspoon dried chives
1 teaspoon salt
* * * * *
1 slice white bread, torn into
   pieces
   Chives, minced

✿ Low Calorie
♥ Low Cholesterol
Servings: 4
Per Serving
Calories: 113
Fat: 0.8 g
Sodium: 800 mg
Cholesterol: 0

Combine all ingredients except bread and minced chives in pressure cooker. Close cover securely. Place pressure regulator on vent pipe. COOK 10 MINUTES at 15 pounds pressure. Let pressure drop of its own accord. Process soup mixture and bread in food processor or blender until smooth. Garnish with chives.

Intro
Basics
Appetizers
Soups
and
Stocks
Meats
Poultry
Seafood
Vegetables
Breads
Desserts
Whole
Meal
Magic

Vegetable Oxtail Soup

4 cups water
1 pound oxtails, disjointed
1 (13-ounce) can whole
   tomatoes, undrained, cut up

* * * * *

1 cup sliced celery
½ cup chopped onion
⅓ cup sliced carrot

⅓ cup diced parsnip
⅓ cup diced white turnip
1 bay leaf

* * * * *

1 cup cooked barley or
   rice, warm
Salt
Pepper

❋ *Low Calorie*
❤ *Low Cholesterol*

Servings: 6
Per Serving
Calories: 173
Fat: 1.9 g
Sodium: 135 mg
Cholesterol: 13 mg

Place water, oxtails, and tomatoes with liquid into 6- or 8-quart pressure cooker. Close cover securely. Place pressure regulator on vent pipe. COOK 15 MINUTES at 15 pounds pressure. Quick cool cooker. Add celery, onion, carrot, parsnip, turnip, and bay leaf to pressure cooker. Close cover securely. Place pressure regulator on vent pipe. COOK 5 MINUTES at 15 pounds pressure. Let pressure drop of its own accord. Stir in barley; season to taste with salt and pepper.

● ● ● ● ● ● ●

❋ *Low Calorie*

Servings: 6
Per Serving
Calories: 296
Fat: 18.7 g
Sodium: 716 mg
Cholesterol: 59 mg

(Shown on page 58)

Mexican Chicken and Corn Soup

2 tablespoons vegetable oil
12 ounces boneless skinless
    chicken breasts, cut into
    ¾-inch pieces
1½ cups drained canned or frozen
    (thawed) whole kernel corn
1 cup chopped onion
½ cup chopped green pepper
½ cup chopped red pepper

½-1 small jalapeño chile, seeded,
     deveined, minced
½ teaspoon ground cumin
3 cups chicken stock or broth

* * * * *

1½ cups shredded Monterey
    Jack cheese
¾ cup half-and-half
Salt

Heat oil in pressure cooker over medium heat. Sauté chicken until no longer pink in the center, about 3 minutes. Add corn, onion, green and red pepper, chile, and cumin. Sauté 2 minutes. Stir in chicken stock. Close cover securely. Place pressure regulator on vent pipe. COOK 5 MINUTES at 15 pounds pressure. Let pressure drop of its own accord. Stir in cheese and half-and-half, stirring until cheese is melted. Season to taste with salt.

Lentil Soup with Franks

1 pound dried lentils
¼ cup vegetable oil
1 tablespoon salt
   Water to well cover
   vegetables
4 slices lean beef or turkey
   bacon, diced
1½ cups chopped leeks
½ cup chopped carrot
½ cup chopped celery

2 teaspoons salt
1 teaspoon cumin seeds or
   ground cumin
4 whole cloves
2 bay leaves
   Water

* * * * *

1 pound lean beef or turkey
   frankfurters

Servings: 8
Per Serving
Calories: 389
Fat: 15.5 g
Sodium: 1937 mg
Cholesterol: 34 mg

(Shown on page 160)

Soak lentils overnight in oil, salt, and water to well cover vegetables; drain. Fry bacon in 6- or 8-quart pressure cooker over medium heat until golden. Add leeks, carrot, and celery. Sauté until tender. Stir in lentils, salt, cumin, cloves, and bay leaves. Add enough water to fill pressure cooker half full. Close cover securely. Place pressure regulator on vent pipe. COOK 20 MINUTES at 15 pounds pressure. Let pressure drop of its own accord. Discard bay leaves and cloves. Thinly slice frankfurters. Stir into soup. Heat until hot.

• • • • • • •

Beet Borscht

1 tablespoon vegetable oil
1 pound lean boneless beef,
   cut into 1-inch cubes
5 cups water
2½ cups chopped raw beets
1½ cups chopped onions
½ cup sliced carrot

2 tablespoons tomato paste
2 tablespoons wine vinegar
1 teaspoon dillweed

* * * * *

½ teaspoon salt
⅛ teaspoon pepper
   Sour cream

❀ *Low Calorie*
Servings: 10
Per Serving
Calories: 111
Fat: 4.6 g
Sodium: 172 mg
Cholesterol: 31 mg

(Shown on page 147)

Heat oil in 6- or 8-quart pressure cooker over medium heat. Brown beef. Add water. Heat to boiling. Skim surface. Add beets, onions, carrot, tomato paste, vinegar, and dillweed. Close cover securely. Place pressure regulator on vent pipe. COOK 10 MINUTES at 15 pounds pressure. Let pressure drop of its own accord. Add salt and pepper. Serve with sour cream.

Intro

Basics

Appetizers

Soups
and
Stocks

Meats

Poultry

Seafood

Vegetables

Breads

Desserts

Whole
Meal
Magic

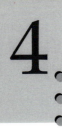

Black Bean Soup

1 cup dried black beans	½ teaspoon dried oregano
2 tablespoons vegetable oil	¼ teaspoon dried thyme
1½ teaspoons salt	1 bay leaf
Water to well cover beans	4 cups chicken stock or broth
1 tablespoon vegetable oil	1 medium tomato
1 cup chopped onion	* * * * *
2-3 cloves garlic, minced	Sour cream or plain yogurt
1 jalapeño chile, seeded, deveined, minced	Cilantro or parsley, minced

 *Low Calorie*

Servings: 6
Per Serving
Calories: 150
Fat: 5.1 g
Sodium: 719 mg
Cholesterol: 0

Soak beans overnight in 2 tablespoons oil, salt, and water to well cover beans; drain. Heat 1 tablespoon oil in pressure cooker over medium heat. Sauté onion, garlic, chile, oregano, thyme, and bay leaf until onion is tender. Stir in beans, chicken stock, and tomato. Close cover securely. Place pressure regulator on vent pipe. COOK 20 MINUTES at 15 pounds pressure. Let pressure drop of its own accord. Discard bay leaf. Process bean mixture in food processor or blender until smooth. Garnish with sour cream and cilantro.

● ● ● ● ● ● ●

Chicken and Okra Gumbo

 *Low Calorie*

Servings: 6
Per Serving
Calories: 126
Fat: 6.1 g
Sodium: 536 mg
Cholesterol: 15 mg

2 tablespoons vegetable oil	1 (16-ounce) can whole tomatoes, undrained, chopped
2 tablespoons all-purpose flour	
½ cup chopped onion	½ cup sliced okra
½ cup chopped green pepper	½ -1 teaspoon red pepper sauce
½ cup thinly sliced celery	1 bay leaf
8 ounces boneless skinless chicken breast, cut into ½-inch pieces	* * * * *
	2 tablespoons filé powder
3 cups chicken stock or broth	Salt

Mix oil and flour in pressure cooker. Cook over medium-high heat, stirring constantly, until mixture is a dark red-brown color. Stir in onion, green pepper, and celery. Cook 3 minutes. Stir in remaining ingredients, except filé powder and salt. Close cover securely. Place pressure regulator on vent pipe. COOK 5 MINUTES at 15 pounds pressure. Let pressure drop of its own accord. Just before serving, stir in filé powder. Season to taste with salt.

French Onion Soup

❋ **Low Calorie**
Servings: 4
Per Serving
Calories: 151
Fat: 8.4 g
Sodium: 779 mg
Cholesterol: 0

2 tablespoons vegetable oil
1 pound yellow onions, thinly sliced
2 cloves garlic, minced
½ teaspoon sugar
1 tablespoon all-purpose flour

½ teaspoon dried thyme
¼ teaspoon pepper
1 bay leaf
4 cups beef stock or broth

* * * * *

Salt

Heat oil in pressure cooker over medium heat. Sauté onions and garlic. Stir in sugar. Cook, uncovered, over medium-low heat until onions are golden. Stir in flour, thyme, pepper, and bay leaf. Cook 1 minute. Stir in beef stock. Close cover securely. Place pressure regulator on vent pipe. COOK 5 MINUTES at 15 pounds pressure. Let pressure drop of its own accord. Season to taste with salt.

● ● ● ● ● ● ●

Curried Corn Soup

Servings: 4
Per Serving
Calories: 343
Fat: 28.5 g
Sodium: 705 mg
Cholesterol: 4 mg

1 tablespoon margarine
1 cup chopped onion
1 jalapeño chile, seeded, deveined, minced
½ teaspoon ground coriander
½ teaspoon ground cumin
½ teaspoon ground turmeric
¼ teaspoon ground cinnamon
½ teaspoon salt

¼ -½ teaspoon pepper
1 cup chicken stock or broth
1 cup drained canned or frozen (thawed) whole kernel corn

* * * * *

1 (14-ounce) can unsweetened coconut milk
1 cup milk
Cilantro or parsley, minced

Heat margarine in pressure cooker over medium heat. Sauté onions and chile until tender. Stir in spices, salt, and pepper. Sauté 1 minute. Stir in chicken stock and corn. Close cover securely. Place pressure regulator on vent pipe. COOK 1 MINUTE at 15 pounds pressure. Let pressure drop of its own accord. Stir in coconut milk and milk. Cook over medium heat, stirring constantly just until hot, 1 to 2 minutes. Sprinkle with cilantro.

Intro

Basics

Appetizers

Soups and Stocks

Meats

Poultry

Seafood

Vegetables

Breads

Desserts

Whole Meal Magic

4.

Hearty Chili

2 pounds coarsely ground beef round	1 teaspoon ground cumin
1 large onion, chopped	1 teaspoon salt
1 green pepper, chopped	½ teaspoon black pepper
1 (8-ounce) can tomato sauce	½ teaspoon dried oregano
2 cups water	¼ teaspoon cayenne pepper
1 tablespoon chili powder	* * * * *
2 cloves garlic, finely chopped	1 (16-ounce) can kidney beans, drained, rinsed

Brown beef, onion, and green pepper in pressure cooker over medium heat. Discard excess fat. Stir in remaining ingredients except beans. Close cover securely. Place pressure regulator on vent pipe. COOK 5 MINUTES at 15 pounds pressure. Let pressure drop of its own accord. Stir in beans. Cook until hot.

NOTE: *If desired, beans can be increased to 2 cans. For hotter chili, increase cayenne pepper and/or chili powder.*

Servings: 8
Per Serving
Calories: 363
Fat: 23.7 g
Sodium: 681 mg
Cholesterol: 84 mg

(Shown on page 58)

Chicken and White Bean Chili

❀ *Low Calorie*
Servings: 4
Per Serving
Calories: 253
Fat: 9.2 g
Sodium: 1105 mg
Cholesterol: 46 mg

1 cup dried great northern beans	½-1 jalapeño chile, seeded, deveined, minced
2 tablespoons vegetable oil	2 teaspoons chili powder
1½ teaspoons salt	1 teaspoon dried oregano
Water to well cover beans	¼ teaspoon ground allspice
1 tablespoon olive or vegetable oil	4 cups chicken stock or broth
1 pound boneless skinless chicken breasts, cut into ¾-inch pieces	1½ teaspoons packed brown sugar
½ cup chopped onion	1 teaspoon white wine vinegar
½ cup sliced carrot	* * * * *
2 cloves garlic, minced	Salt
	Pepper

Soak beans overnight in 2 tablespoons oil, 1½ teaspoons salt, and water to well cover beans; drain. Heat olive oil in pressure cooker over medium heat. Sauté chicken until no longer pink in the center, about 3 minutes. Add onion, carrot, garlic, chile, chili powder, oregano, and allspice. Sauté 2 minutes. Stir in beans, chicken stock, brown sugar, and vinegar. Close cover securely. Place pressure regulator on vent pipe. COOK 20 MINUTES at 15 pounds pressure. Let pressure drop of its own accord. Season to taste with salt and pepper.

Chilled Spinach Soup

2 cups turkey, chicken, or beef
   stock or broth
2 cups fresh spinach
1 large white potato, sliced

* * * * *

½ cup sour cream
Salt
Pepper

❋ *Low Calorie*
Servings: 8
Per Serving
Calories: 58
Fat: 3.4 g
Sodium: 214 mg
Cholesterol: 6 mg

Combine broth, spinach, and potato in pressure cooker. Close cover securely. Place pressure regulator on vent pipe. COOK 5 MINUTES at 15 pounds pressure. Let pressure drop of its own accord. Cool soup to room temperature. Process in food processor or blender until smooth. Stir in sour cream. Season to taste with salt and pepper. Refrigerate until chilled.

Mulligatawny Soup

2 tablespoons vegetable oil
1 pound boneless skinless
   chicken breasts, cut into
   ¾-inch pieces
½ cup chopped green pepper
½ cup chopped onion
2 tablespoons all-purpose flour
1 teaspoon curry powder
¼ teaspoon ground nutmeg
2 whole cloves

2 quarts chicken stock or broth
1 cup chopped tomato
¾ cup chopped carrot

* * * * *

¼-½ cup whipping cream or
   half-and-half
Salt
White pepper
Paprika

❋ *Low Calorie*
Servings: 8
Per Serving
Calories: 155
Fat: 8.2 g
Sodium: 804 mg
Cholesterol: 31 mg

Heat oil in 6- or 8-quart pressure cooker over medium heat. Sauté chicken until browned and no longer pink in the center, about 5 minutes. Remove chicken and reserve. Add green pepper and onion to pressure cooker. Sauté until tender. Stir in flour, curry powder, nutmeg, and cloves. Cook 1 minute. Add chicken stock, tomato, and carrot. Close cover securely. Place pressure regulator on vent pipe. COOK 5 MINUTES at 15 pounds pressure. Let pressure drop of its own accord. Discard cloves. Process soup mixture in blender or food processor until smooth. Return to pressure cooker. Stir in cream and reserved chicken. Cook over medium heat, just until hot, 1 to 2 minutes. Season to taste with salt and pepper. Sprinkle with paprika.

Intro

Basics

Appetizers

Soups
and
Stocks

Meats

Poultry

Seafood

Vegetables

Breads

Desserts

Whole
Meal
Magic

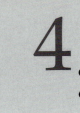

Potato-Leek Soup

1 tablespoon margarine	⅓ cup whipping cream or half-and-half
1½ cups chopped leeks	
1 tablespoon all-purpose flour	2 tablespoons chopped dill pickle
4 cups chicken stock or broth	Salt
4 cups diced peeled potatoes	Pepper

* * * * *

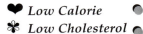 Low Calorie
Low Cholesterol

Servings: 8
Per Serving
Calories: 166
Fat: 5.4 g
Sodium: 537 mg
Cholesterol: 11 mg

Heat margarine in pressure cooker over medium heat. Sauté leeks until tender. Stir in flour. Cook 1 minute. Stir in chicken stock and potatoes. Close cover securely. Place pressure regulator on vent pipe. COOK 4 MINUTES at 15 pounds pressure. Let pressure drop of its own accord. Stir in cream and pickle. Heat just until hot. Season to taste with salt and pepper.

● ● ● ● ● ● ●

Brussels Sprouts Soup

Low Calorie

Servings: 4
Per Serving
Calories: 152
Fat: 6.5 g
Sodium: 148 mg
Cholesterol: 1 mg

1 cup water	1¾ cups skim milk
1 pound brussels sprouts, trimmed	½ teaspoon onion powder
	Salt
* * * * *	White pepper
2 tablespoons margarine	Ground nutmeg
2 tablespoons all-purpose flour	

Place cooking rack (or basket) and water in pressure cooker. Place brussels sprouts on rack (or in basket). Close cover securely. Place pressure regulator on vent pipe. COOK 3 MINUTES at 15 pounds pressure. Quick cool cooker. Drain brussels sprouts. Process in food processor or blender until smooth. Heat margarine in pressure cooker over medium heat. Stir in flour and cook until smooth. Stir in milk. Heat to boiling. Simmer, stirring constantly, 1 minute. Stir in onion powder and puréed sprouts. Season to taste with salt and pepper. Sprinkle lightly with nutmeg.

Vegetable Soup

❋ *Low Calorie*
Servings: 6
Per Serving
Calories: 171
Fat: 6 g
Sodium: 163 mg
Cholesterol: 48 mg

1 tablespoon vegetable oil
1 pound beef, cut into 1-inch cubes
4 cups water
1 (13-ounce) can whole tomatoes, undrained, cut up

* * * * *

1 cup sliced celery
½ cup chopped onion
⅓ cup sliced carrot
⅓ cup diced parsnip
⅓ cup diced white turnip
⅓ cup peeled and cubed potatoes
1 cup shredded cabbage

Heat oil in 6- or 8-quart pressure cooker over medium heat. Brown beef. Add water and tomatoes. Close cover securely. Place pressure regulator on vent pipe. COOK 15 MINUTES at 15 pounds pressure. Let pressure drop of its own accord. Add remaining ingredients. COOK 5 MINUTES at 15 pounds pressure. Let pressure drop of its own accord.

Country Cabbage Soup

❋ *Low Calorie*
Servings: 8
Per Serving
Calories: 72
Fat: 3.2 g
Sodium: 502 mg
Cholesterol: 11 mg

1 (13¾-ounce) can chicken broth (1¼ cup) or stock
2 cups water
1 teaspoon salt
½ teaspoon freshly ground black pepper
2 pounds meaty pork bones (excess fat removed)

* * * * *

1 pound cabbage, shredded
1 cup chopped onion
½ cup chopped fresh tomato
2 teaspoons paprika
1 (4-ounce) can sliced mushrooms, including liquid
2 cups water

Combine chicken broth, 2 cups water, salt, pepper, and pork in 6- or 8-quart pressure cooker. Close cover securely. Place pressure regulator on vent pipe. COOK 30 MINUTES at 15 pounds pressure. Let pressure drop of its own accord. Reserve liquid. Set meat aside to cool. When cool, remove meat from bones and add to reserved liquid. This may be done a day ahead. When ready to prepare soup, put meat and reserved broth in pressure cooker. Add cabbage, onion, tomato, paprika, mushrooms, and 2 cups water to meat mixture. Close cover securely. Place pressure regulator on vent pipe. COOK 5 MINUTES at 15 pounds pressure. Let pressure drop of its own accord.

Intro

Basics

Appetizers

Soups
and
Stocks

Meats

Poultry

Seafood

Vegetables

Breads

Desserts

Whole
Meal
Magic

4.

Vegetarian Pea Soup

1 cup dried whole green or yellow peas	1 bay leaf, crumbled
2 tablespoons vegetable oil	2 tablespoons chopped green pepper
1½ teaspoons salt	2 tablespoons chopped carrot
Water to well cover peas	½ cup diced celery
5 vegetable bouillon cubes	1 onion, chopped
⅛ teaspoon black pepper	6 cups water
1 teaspoon salt	

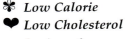

Low Calorie
Low Cholesterol

Servings: 6
Per Serving
Calories: 144
Fat: 2.1 g
Sodium: 1268 mg
Cholesterol: 0

Soak peas overnight in oil, salt, and enough water to well cover peas. Drain and discard liquid. Place peas and remaining ingredients in pressure cooker. Close cover securely. Place pressure regulator on vent pipe. COOK 5 MINUTES at 15 pounds pressure. Let pressure drop of its own accord.

NOTE: To make Pea Soup with Ham, add 1 cup cut-up leftover ham.

● ● ● ● ● ● ●

Low Cholesterol
Servings: 4
Per Serving
Calories: 339
Fat: 8.5 g
Sodium: 380 mg
Cholesterol: 77 mg

Beef Soup, New Orleans Style

1 pound soup meat, diced	2 cups stewed tomatoes
1 small soup bone	✳ ✳ ✳ ✳ ✳
3 cups water	1 cup cooked corn
1 large onion, chopped	1 cup chopped okra
3 large tomatoes, peeled and chopped	½ cup cooked rice
½ green pepper, chopped	⅛ teaspoon cayenne pepper
2 cloves garlic, minced	Salt
	Pepper

Place soup meat, soup bone, water, onion, tomatoes, green pepper, garlic, and stewed tomatoes in pressure cooker. Close cover securely. Place pressure regulator on vent pipe. COOK 20 MINUTES at 15 pounds pressure. Let pressure drop of its own accord. Remove soup bone. Add remaining ingredients. Close cover securely. Place pressure regulator on vent pipe. COOK 0 MINUTES. Let pressure drop of its own accord.

NOTE: Fresh tomatoes provide attractive chunks, canned tomatoes provide juice.

Bouillabaisse

⅓ cup olive or vegetable oil
3 medium onions, chopped
½ cup chopped green bell pepper
2 cloves garlic, minced
½ teaspoon minced parsley
1 (35-ounce) can Italian peeled tomatoes, chopped, with liquid
2 cups dry red wine
1 bay leaf
½ teaspoon basil
1 teaspoon oregano
1 pound medium shrimp, shelled and deveined, with the tail intact, or 1 (1-pound) package frozen shelled and deveined shrimp
1 pound firm white fish fillets, such as sea bass, striped bass or scrod, cut into 2½- x 2-inch pieces
6 cherrystone or littleneck clams, well scrubbed, optional

* * * * *

Salt
Pepper

Servings: 6
Per Serving
Calories: 360
Fat: 14.7 g
Sodium: 460 mg
Cholesterol: 147 mg

Heat oil in 6- or 8-quart pressure cooker over medium heat. Sauté onions, green pepper, and garlic until golden brown. Add remaining ingredients. Close cover securely. Place pressure regulator on vent pipe. COOK 3 MINUTES at 15 pounds pressure. Let pressure drop of its own accord. Season to taste with salt and pepper.

●　●　●　●　●　●　●

New England Clam Chowder

4 slices bacon, chopped
2 cups chopped onions
4 cups cubed potatoes
2 teaspoons salt
⅛ teaspoon pepper
2 cups water

* * * * *

2 (8-ounce) cans minced clams
1 quart light cream
¼ cup butter

Servings: 8
Per Serving
Calories: 460
Fat: 31.6 g
Sodium: 756 mg
Cholesterol: 135 mg

Sauté bacon and onions in pressure cooker over medium heat. Add potatoes, salt, pepper, and water. Close cover securely. Place pressure regulator on vent pipe. COOK 5 MINUTES at 15 pounds pressure. Let pressure drop of its own accord. Drain clams. Slowly add clams, 1 cup clam liquid, cream, and butter. Stir constantly. Simmer 10 minutes in open pressure cooker.

Intro

Basics

Appetizers

Soups
and
Stocks

Meats

Poultry

Seafood

Vegetables

Breads

Desserts

Whole
Meal
Magic

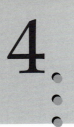

Hot-Sour Soup

4	dried Chinese black mushrooms	1½	tablespoons light soy sauce
1	dried cloud ear, optional	2-3	tablespoons Chinese rice or white wine vinegar
	Hot water	1	tablespoon sesame seed oil
4	cups chicken stock	½	teaspoon sugar
½	cup diced firm bean curd (scant ½-inch dice)	½-¾	teaspoon white pepper

4 dried Chinese black mushrooms

1 dried cloud ear, optional
  Hot water

4 cups chicken stock

½ cup diced firm bean curd (scant ½-inch dice)

⅓ cup shredded bamboo shoots

8 medium shrimp, peeled, deveined, cut lengthwise into halves

3 tablespoons cornstarch mixed with ½ cup cold water

1½ tablespoons light soy sauce

2-3 tablespoons Chinese rice or white wine vinegar

1 tablespoon sesame seed oil

½ teaspoon sugar

½-¾ teaspoon white pepper

* * * * *

1 (7-ounce) can baby corn, drained, cut lengthwise into fourths

2 egg whites
  Green onions, sliced
  Cilantro or parsley, minced

❋ Low Calorie

Servings: 6

Per Serving
Calories: 148
Fat: 5.6 g
Sodium: 799 mg
Cholesterol: 14 mg

Soak mushrooms in hot water until softened, 15 to 20 minutes. Drain and slice, discarding any tough centers or stems. Place mushrooms and remaining ingredients except corn, egg whites, green onions, and cilantro in 6- or 8-quart pressure cooker. Close cover securely. Place pressure regulator on vent pipe. COOK 0 MINUTES. Let pressure drop of its own accord. Remove cover. Add corn. Stir egg whites slowly into soup. Heat for 2 minutes. Serve soup in bowls; sprinkle with green onions and cilantro.

NOTE: Chinese mushrooms can be purchased in Oriental groceries and in the specialty departments of large supermarkets.

Manhattan Seafood Stew

1 (1-pound) package frozen
  cod fillets
1 (8-ounce) package frozen
  baby lobster tails or 2
  medium lobster tails or
  1 (6-ounce) package
  frozen shrimp in shell*
2 tablespoons olive oil
1 onion, chopped
1 leek, chopped
2 cloves garlic, minced
2 medium tomatoes, peeled,
  chopped

1 cup fish stock or bottled
  clam juice
1 teaspoon dried Italian herbs
½ teaspoon fennel seeds
  Pinch saffron

* * * * *

8 clams or mussels in shell,
  cleaned, optional

* * * * *

Salt
Pepper

♥ Low Calorie
✿ Low Cholesterol
Servings: 6
Per Serving
Calories: 200
Fat: 6.1 g
Sodium: 188 mg
Cholesterol: 69 mg

Let fish stand at room temperature 15 to 20 minutes. Cut fish block into 4 even pieces. If using medium lobster tails, let stand at room temperature 15 to 20 minutes; cut each into 2 or 3 pieces. Heat oil in pressure cooker over medium heat. Sauté onion, leek, and garlic until tender. Add tomatoes, fish stock, Italian herbs, fennel seeds, and saffron. Add frozen fish and lobster tails. (If using shrimp, do not add at this point.) Close cover securely. Place pressure regulator on vent pipe. COOK 5 MINUTES at 15 pounds pressure. Quick cool cooker. Add shrimp, if using, and clams. Close cover securely. Place pressure regulator on vent pipe. COOK 3 MINUTES at 15 pounds pressure. Let pressure drop of its own accord. Season to taste with salt and pepper.

*For easier eating, lobster or shrimp may be shelled.

Intro

Basics

Appetizers

Soups
and
Stocks

Meats

Poultry

Seafood

Vegetables

Breads

Desserts

Whole
Meal
Magic

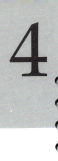

Vegetable Stock

1 tablespoon vegetable oil	½ cup sliced zucchini
½ cup chopped onion	½ cup sliced mushrooms
1 clove garlic, minced	½ cup green beans
½ cup chopped carrot	½ cup chopped tomato
½ cup sliced celery	6 sprigs parsley
½ cup chopped parsnip	1 teaspoon salt
3 cups water	½ teaspoon dried thyme
½ cup sliced yellow summer squash	2 bay leaves

❋ *Low Calorie*

Servings: 3¼ cups
Per Serving (per cup)
Calories: 43
Fat: 4.2 g
Sodium: 659 mg
Cholesterol: 0

Heat oil in pressure cooker over medium heat. Sauté onion and garlic until tender. Add carrot, celery, and parsnip. Sauté 2 minutes. Add remaining ingredients. Close cover securely. Place pressure regulator on vent pipe. COOK 10 MINUTES at 15 pounds pressure. Let pressure drop of its own accord. Strain stock, discarding solids.

❋ *Low Calorie*
♥ *Low Cholesterol*

Servings: 5 cups
Per Serving (per cup)
Calories: 44
Fat: 0.5 g
Sodium: 220 mg
Cholesterol: 5 mg

Fish Stock

1 pound whole whitefish, including bones and head, cleaned, cut into 2-inch pieces (sole, cod, orange roughy, or halibut)	1 medium onion, cut into 1-inch pieces
	1 clove garlic, optional
	½ teaspoon dried tarragon
3 cups water	½ teaspoon salt
1 cup dry white wine or water	¼ teaspoon celery seeds
1 medium carrot, cut into 1-inch pieces	3 whole peppercorns
	1 large sprig parsley
	1 bay leaf

Combine all ingredients in pressure cooker. Close cover securely. Place pressure regulator on vent pipe. COOK 20 MINUTES at 15 pounds pressure. Let pressure drop of its own accord. Strain stock, discarding solids.

Chicken Stock

1 (3- to 3½-pound) chicken, cut up
4 cups water
½ cup chopped carrot
½ cup chopped onion
¼ cup chopped celery
1 teaspoon salt
2 sprigs parsley
2 whole peppercorns

❋ *Low Calorie*
Servings: 4½ cups
Per Serving *(per cup)*
Calories: 33
Fat: 1.7 g
Sodium: 481 mg
Cholesterol: 12 mg

Combine all ingredients in pressure cooker. Close cover securely. Place pressure regulator on vent pipe. COOK 15 MINUTES at 15 pounds pressure. Let pressure drop of its own accord. Strain stock, discarding solids. Skim off fat and discard.

Beef Stock

1 tablespoon vegetable oil
1 pound beef cubes for stew
½ pound cracked beef bones
4 cups water
½ cup chopped onion
¼ cup chopped carrot
¼ cup sliced celery
1 teaspoon salt
1 sprig parsley
¼ teaspoon dried thyme
¼ teaspoon dried marjoram
8 whole peppercorns

❋ *Low Calorie*
Servings: 3¼ cups
Per Serving *(per cup)*
Calories: 64
Fat: 5.7 g
Sodium: 661 mg
Cholesterol: 10 mg

Heat oil in pressure cooker over medium heat. Brown beef cubes and bones. Add remaining ingredients. Close cover securely. Place pressure regulator on vent pipe. COOK 15 MINUTES at 15 pounds pressure. Let pressure drop of its own accord. Strain stock, discarding solids. Skim off fat and discard.

Intro

Basics

Appetizers

Soups and Stocks

Meats

Poultry

Seafood

Vegetables

Breads

Desserts

Whole Meal Magic

Notes

Sweet 'n Sour Chicken...Page 101

Coconut Custards...Page 171

49

Stuffed Apples...Page 174

Napa Valley Chops...Page 67

50

Shrimp-Stuffed Artichokes...Page 22

Vegetables with Curried Dill Dip...Page 28

51

Chinese Chicken Salad...Page 110

Chilorio...Page 82

Steamed Zucchini Bread...Page 164

54

Brown Rice with Veggies...Page 141

Ruby Pears...Page 172

Salmon Steaks Moutarde...Page 117

Chicken with Cracked Pepper...Page 98

Company Beef Roast with Gravy...Page 70

Petite Pumpkin Custards...Page 169

Savory Rice Stuffed Onions...Page 142

Lentil Soup with Franks...Page 35

Minestrone...Page 33

Hearty Chili...Page 38

Mexican Chicken and Corn Soup...Page 34

Arroz Con Pollo...Page 107

59

Country Captain Chicken...Page 99

Apricot Barbecue Pork Roast...Page 74

Saffron Fish Stew...Page 115

63

Roots with Ginger Sauce...Page 140

5. Meats

"...magically tenderizes even extra-lean budget cuts in minutes."

Americans have always been meat lovers. Even back in the forties when budget-minded cooks shook their heads over high meat prices—*25 to 45 cents a pound!*—they still served "meat and potatoes" meals practically every day. With wartime meat rationing, they made do with variety meats, like oxtail, and discovered new stews and unusual casseroles that fed many mouths from just a few ounces of meat.

When the war ended, beef steak was back on the menu along with thick ham steak, no longer sliced according to how many meat stamps the buyer had to spend. Then the informal eating styles of the fifties catapulted outdoor meat grilling to a new high. Hamburgers, ribs, shish kabobs, chops, and even roasts got the weekend charcoal treatment, usually with Dad wearing the apron.

Foreign cuisines were exerting a new influence over American main dishes. In the sixties, sauerbraten, goulash, steak au poivre, sukiyaki, and Beef Wellington came out of the restaurants and into the home kitchen.

5.

When the country's collective nutritional consciousness began to be raised in the seventies, meat got a bad reputation. Technology responded with textured soy products used as no-fat, no-cholesterol meat extenders and even as 100% imitation meat products. The trouble was that most folks thought these prime fakes had no taste, so real meat remained solidly front and center on the menu.

Over the next decade, consumers slowly learned more about the complex relationship between diet and health. They learned that the connection between what we eat and how we look and feel is a function, not of specific foods but of our total eating habits over time. Variety is the key to eating right—and that can include red meats.

Nowadays, meat is downplayed with larger roles going to whole grains, legumes, and vegetables. We combine meats with other good foods to savor the taste without sacrificing what's in our best nutritional interest. We choose leaner cuts and give a lot of thought to selecting cooking methods that contribute to eating light.

Pressure cooking is the best choice, bar none! It is virtually fat-free because super-heated steam, not fat, cooks the food. You can even skip initial browning for most recipes, since pressure cooking so thoroughly brings out every bit of robust flavor. Pressure cooking magically tenderizes even extra-lean budget cuts in minutes.

The next several pages will tempt your taste buds with fast and easy pressure cooking recipes for all your favorite meats. Time-honored favorites, like *Company Beef Roast* and *Colonial Boiled Dinner*, share the bill with delightful new ethnic dishes and regional specialties—*Osso Buco*; *Indian Lamb Curry*; *Spicy Sausage, Red Beans and Rice*; and *Picadillo* (a zesty filling you can use for authentic-tasting tacos, burritos, and enchiladas).

Barbecued Beef for Sandwiches

1 tablespoon vegetable oil
3 pound boneless beef rump roast
1 large onion, sliced
1½ cups catsup
1½ cups water
½ cup cider vinegar
⅓ cup packed brown sugar
2 tablespoons Worcestershire sauce

1 teaspoon paprika
1 teaspoon chili powder
½ teaspoon salt
½ teaspoon garlic powder
½ teaspoon liquid smoke
⅛ teaspoon cayenne pepper

* * * * *

2 tablespoons cornstarch, optional
Cold water, optional

❀ *Low Calorie*
Servings: 16
Per Serving
Calories: 188
Fat: 6.7 g
Sodium: 385 mg
Cholesterol: 58 mg

Heat oil in pressure cooker over medium heat. Brown roast on all sides. Remove roast. Combine remaining ingredients, except cornstarch and water. Place cooking rack (or basket) and combined ingredients in pressure cooker. Place roast on rack (or in basket). Close cover securely. Place pressure regulator on vent pipe. COOK 35 MINUTES at 15 pounds pressure. Let pressure drop of its own accord. Remove roast and rack (or basket). Cook onion and sauce until thickened, stirring constantly. Sauce may be thickened with a mixture of cornstarch mixed with cold water, if desired. Slice roast and serve in or with sauce. For sandwiches, use buns, French bread, or pita bread pockets. Or serve barbecued beef on top of cornbread or cooked grits.

● ● ● ● ● ● ●

Napa Valley Chops

1-2 tablespoons vegetable oil
1 small onion, chopped
4 pork chops, 1 inch thick, trimmed
1 cup beef stock or broth
½ cup dry red wine

½ teaspoon dried thyme
½ teaspoon sugar
½ teaspoon salt

* * * * *

1⅓ cups instant rice

❀ *Low Calorie*
Servings: 4
Per Serving
Calories: 298
Fat: 13.9 g
Sodium: 449 mg
Cholesterol: 63 mg

(Shown on page 50)

Heat oil in pressure cooker over medium heat. Sauté onion until tender. Remove onion and reserve. Brown chops on both sides, adding more oil if needed. Arrange chops in single layer in pressure cooker. Add beef stock, wine, thyme, sugar, salt, and reserved onion. Close cover securely. Place pressure regulator on vent pipe. COOK 9 MINUTES at 15 pounds pressure. Quick cool cooker. Remove chops. Keep warm. Measure cooking liquid in pressure cooker. Add boiling water, if needed, to measure 1⅓ cups. Stir in rice. Let stand 5 minutes. Serve rice with chops.

Intro

Basics

Appetizers

Soups and Stocks

Meats

Poultry

Seafood

Vegetables

Breads

Desserts

Whole Meal Magic

67

5.

Beef Roast in Wine with Julienne Vegetables

3 pound boneless beef rump
  roast
Salt
Pepper
2 tablespoons vegetable oil
1 cup chopped onion
¾ cup dry red wine
2 cups water

* * * * *
¾-1 cup each julienne-cut carrots,
  celery, green beans, and
  turnips
* * * * *
1 tablespoon all-purpose flour
2 tablespoons cold water

Servings: 8
Per Serving
Calories: 345
Fat: 15.2 g
Sodium: 84 mg
Cholesterol: 116 mg

Sprinkle roast with salt and pepper. Heat oil in pressure cooker over medium heat. Brown roast. Add onion. Cook until brown. Stir in wine and 2 cups water. Close cover securely. Place pressure regulator on vent pipe. COOK 35 MINUTES at 15 pounds pressure. Quick cool cooker. Open pressure cooker. Place cooking rack (or basket) on top of roast. Place vegetables in 4 individual foil boats. Place boats on rack (or in basket). Close cover securely. Place pressure regulator on vent pipe. COOK 0 MINUTES. Let pressure drop of its own accord. Remove vegetables, rack (or basket), and roast from pressure cooker. Keep warm. Mix 1 tablespoon flour with cold water. Stir into wine mixture in pressure cooker. Cook and stir until gravy boils and thickens. Serve with roast.

● ● ● ● ● ● ●

❀ *Low Calorie*
Servings: 10
Per Serving
Calories: 221
Fat: 8.7 g
Sodium: 61 mg
Cholesterol: 62 mg

Country-Style Brisket

2½ cups water
2 pound beef brisket, trimmed
* * * * *
4 medium potatoes, unpared,
  cut into ¾-inch pieces
4 large carrots, cut into 2-inch
  pieces

* * * * *
Salt
Pepper
Minced parsley
Horseradish sauce

Place cooking rack (or basket) and water in pressure cooker. Place brisket on rack (or in basket). Close cover securely. Place pressure regulator on vent pipe. COOK 30 MINUTES at 15 pounds pressure. Let pressure drop of its own accord. Add potatoes and carrots to pressure cooker. Close cover securely. Place pressure regulator on vent pipe. COOK 2 MINUTES at 15 pounds pressure. Let pressure drop of its own accord. Arrange beef and vegetables on platter. Sprinkle vegetables lightly with salt, pepper, and parsley. Serve with horseradish sauce.

Hot-Sour Pork with Tofu

❀ Low Calorie
Servings: 6
Per Serving
Calories: 174
Fat: 10.8 g
Sodium: 444 mg
Cholesterol: 20 mg

1 (6- to 8-ounce) pork tenderloin, trimmed
2 tablespoons vegetable oil
8 mushrooms, sliced
1 cup chicken stock or broth
½ cup water
1 teaspoon grated fresh ginger or ½ teaspoon ground ginger
1 clove garlic, minced
½ teaspoon salt

1 tablespoon chopped pimiento
2 teaspoons white wine vinegar
2 teaspoons soy sauce
1½ teaspoons sugar
¼-½ teaspoon crushed red pepper
2 teaspoons cornstarch
1 tablespoon water
12 ounces tofu, cut into ½-inch cubes (2 cups)
Hot cooked rice or chow mein noodles

* * * * *

Cut pork into 1½- x ¼-inch strips. Heat oil in pressure cooker over medium heat. Stir-fry pork 1 minute. Add mushrooms. Stir-fry 1 minute. Add chicken stock, water, ginger, garlic, and salt. Close cover securely. Place pressure regulator on vent pipe. COOK 5 MINUTES at 15 pounds pressure. Quick cool cooker. Add pimiento, vinegar, soy sauce, sugar, and red pepper to pork. Mix cornstarch with water. Stir into pork mixture. Cook and stir until sauce boils and thickens. Gently fold in tofu. Cook just until hot. Serve over rice or chow mein noodles.

● ● ● ● ● ● ●

Burgundy Beef Stew

❀ Low Calorie
Servings: 6
Per Serving
Calories: 294
Fat: 8.3 g
Sodium: 437 mg
Cholesterol: 98 mg

2 slices thick-sliced bacon, diced
2 pounds boneless lean beef round, cut into 1-inch cubes
½ cup chopped onion
1 large clove garlic, minced
1½ cups red burgundy wine
½ cup water
¾ teaspoon dried thyme
¾ teaspoon salt

¼ teaspoon pepper
1 bay leaf

* * * * *

1 tablespoon tomato paste
½ pound small fresh mushrooms, sautéed
½ pound pearl onions, cooked or 1 (1-pound) can onions, drained

Fry bacon in pressure cooker over medium heat until crisp. Remove bacon and reserve. Brown beef in bacon fat, about one-third at a time. Return all beef to pressure cooker. Add chopped onion and garlic. Cook and stir 2 minutes. Add wine, water, thyme, salt, pepper, and bay leaf. Close cover securely. Place pressure regulator on vent pipe. COOK 15 MINUTES at 15 pounds pressure. Quick cool cooker. Stir in tomato paste, mushrooms, pearl onions, and reserved bacon. Simmer to desired thickness.

Intro

Basics

Appetizers

Soups
and
Stocks

Meats

Poultry

Seafood

Vegetables

Breads

Desserts

Whole
Meal
Magic

5.

Company Beef Roast with Gravy

2 **tablespoons vegetable oil**	1 **medium sweet Spanish**
3 **pound boneless beef rump,**	**onion, cut into wedges,**
bottom round, eye of round	**separated**
or chuck roast	* * * * *
¾ **cup teriyaki sauce**	3 **tablespoons all-purpose flour**
2 **cups water**	¼ **cup water**

Heat oil in pressure cooker over medium heat. Lightly brown roast on all sides. Remove roast. Place cooking rack (or basket), teriyaki sauce, and 2 cups water in pressure cooker. Place roast on rack (or in basket). Arrange onion evenly on top of roast. Close cover securely. Place pressure regulator on vent pipe. Cook, at 15 pounds pressure, for following degrees of doneness: 8-10 MINUTES **per pound** for rare; 10-12 MINUTES **per pound** for medium; AT LEAST 12-15 MINUTES **per pound** for well-done. Let pressure drop of its own accord. Remove roast and rack (or basket) from pressure cooker. Keep warm. Pour drippings into 4-cup measure. Skim off fat. Add enough water to drippings to measure 2½ cups. Mix flour with ¼ cup water. Combine with drippings in pressure cooker. Cook and stir until gravy boils and thickens. Serve gravy with roast.

● ● ● ● ● ● ●

Beef Birds

2 **pounds boneless beef round**	2 **tablespoons chopped parsley**
steak, ¼ inch thick	**All-purpose flour**
1 **small onion, finely chopped**	2 **tablespoons vegetable oil**
2 **teaspoons butter or margarine**	1 **(13¾-ounce) can single-**
1 **cup fresh bread crumbs**	**strength beef broth**
1 **(4¼-ounce) can deviled ham**	1 **clove garlic, minced**
or ½ cup ground ham	1 **teaspoon dried thyme**
1 **egg**	* * * * *
½ **teaspoon dried summer**	**Hot cooked noodles**
savory	

Cut beef into 12 even-sized pieces. Pound lightly for easier rolling. Sauté onion in butter in pressure cooker over medium heat until tender. Combine bread crumbs, ham, egg, savory, and parsley. Place rounded tablespoon of mixture on each piece of steak. Spread slightly. Roll up steak and tie or secure with wooden picks. Coat with flour. Heat oil in pressure cooker over medium heat. Brown beef rolls, a few at a time, and remove. Add beef broth, garlic, and thyme to drippings. Mix well. Return beef rolls to pressure cooker. Close cover securely. Place pressure regulator on vent pipe. COOK 10 MINUTES at 15 pounds pressure. Let pressure drop of its own accord. Serve with noodles.

Apple Country Pork Roast

Servings: 8
Per Serving
Calories: 305
Fat: 13.5 g
Sodium: 1068 mg
Cholesterol: 77 mg

1 tablespoon vegetable oil
3 pound boneless rolled pork loin roast
1 medium onion, sliced
2 celery ribs, cleaned and sliced
2½ cups apple juice
½ cup water

⅓ cup soy sauce

* * * * *

2 envelopes light or regular gravy mix*
1 large tart apple, pared, cored, and finely chopped

Heat oil in pressure cooker over medium heat. Brown roast well on all sides. Remove from cooker. Add onion and celery to cooker; cook and stir until lightly browned. Remove from cooker. Combine apple juice, water, and soy sauce. Add a small amount to cooker, stirring to blend with pan juices. Place cooking rack (or basket) in pressure cooker. Pour in remaining apple juice mixture. Place roast on rack (or in basket); add onion mixture. Close cover securely. Place pressure regulator on vent pipe. COOK 60 MINUTES at 15 pounds pressure. Let pressure drop of its own accord. Remove roast and rack (or basket). Pour out cooking liquid. Strain and remove excess fat, if necessary. Measure 3½ cups cooking liquid. Pour gravy mix into cooker; stir in small amount of cooking liquid. Add remaining liquid and apples. Cook and stir about 1 minute, or until mixture thickens. Serve gravy with roast.

* If desired, gravy mix may be omitted and cooking liquid thickened.

● ● ● ● ● ● ●

Colonial Boiled Dinner

Servings: 8
Per Serving
Calories: 403
Fat: 16.4 g
Sodium: 433 mg
Cholesterol: 117 mg

3 pound beef brisket
½ cup teriyaki sauce
2½ cups water

* * * * *

3-4 small red-skinned potatoes, unpared
2 cups sliced pared turnips

3-4 carrots, pared, cut into quarters
2 large sweet Spanish onions, cut into quarters
1 pound green cabbage, cut into 6 to 8 wedges

Place brisket and teriyaki sauce in plastic bag or glass dish. Close bag securely or cover dish. Marinate in refrigerator for 1 to 2 days, turning frequently. Place cooking rack (or basket) and water in 6- or 8-quart pressure cooker. Place brisket on rack (or in basket), discarding marinade. Close cover securely. Place pressure regulator on vent pipe. COOK 40 MINUTES at 15 pounds pressure. Let pressure drop of its own accord. Remove brisket. Keep warm. Place vegetables on rack (or in basket). Close cover securely. Place pressure regulator on vent pipe. COOK 3 MINUTES at 15 pounds pressure. Quick cool cooker. Thinly slice brisket. Serve with vegetables.

Intro

Basics

Appetizers

Soups and Stocks

Meats

Poultry

Seafood

Vegetables

Breads

Desserts

Whole Meal Magic

5.

Daube of Beef

- 1 (4- to 4½-pound) rolled beef rump roast
- ½ teaspoon soy sauce
- 1 (8-ounce) bottle Light Russian or French salad dressing
- 1½ cups water
- 4 green onions, trimmed
- 1 large clove garlic
- ¼ teaspoon salt
- ¼ teaspoon pepper

Servings: 8
Per Serving
Calories: 314
Fat: 12.9 g
Sodium: 432 mg
Cholesterol: 118 mg

(Shown on page 154)

Pierce roast thoroughly on all sides with long-tined fork. Rub with soy sauce. Place roast and salad dressing in plastic bag or glass dish. Close bag securely or cover dish. Marinate in refrigerator 1 hour or overnight, turning occasionally. Place cooking rack (or basket), water, and marinade in 6- or 8-quart pressure cooker. Place roast on rack (or in basket). Add green onions and garlic. Sprinkle with salt and pepper. Close cover securely. Place pressure regulator on vent pipe. COOK 35 MINUTES at 15 pounds pressure. Let pressure drop of its own accord. Remove roast. Serve at room temperature or chilled.

Indian Lamb Curry

✽ ***Low Calorie***
Servings: 6
Per Serving
Calories: 199
Fat: 9.4 g
Sodium: 483 mg
Cholesterol: 59 mg

- ½ cup plain low-fat yogurt
- ¾ teaspoon salt
- ⅛ teaspoon crushed red pepper
- 1½ pounds lean boneless lamb, cut into 1-inch cubes
- ¼ cup margarine
- 1 tablespoon finely chopped fresh ginger
- 1 clove garlic, minced
- 1 teaspoon crushed coriander seed
- ½ teaspoon ground turmeric
- ½ teaspoon crushed cumin seeds
- ¼ teaspoon ground cinnamon
- ¼ teaspoon black pepper
- ⅛ teaspoon crushed cardamom seed
- 1 cup chopped onion
- ½ cup chicken stock or broth
- 1 cup water

* * * * *

- ¼ cup plain low-fat yogurt
- 2 tablespoons all-purpose flour
- Onion rings
- Lemon wedges

Mix ½ cup yogurt, salt, and red pepper in medium bowl. Stir in lamb. Refrigerate at least 3 hours but no longer than 24 hours. Heat margarine in pressure cooker over medium heat. Stir in ginger, garlic, coriander, turmeric, cumin, cinnamon, black pepper, and cardamom. Cook over low heat 2 minutes. Stir in chopped onion, chicken stock, water, and marinated lamb mixture. Close cover securely. Place pressure regulator on vent pipe. COOK 10 MINUTES at 15 pounds pressure. Let pressure drop of its own accord. Mix ¼ cup yogurt and flour. Stir into lamb mixture. Cook and stir over low heat 3 to 4 minutes. Garnish with onion rings and lemon wedges.

Paprika and Pepper Short Ribs

2-4 tablespoons vegetable oil
3 pounds beef short ribs, trimmed
2 onions, chopped
3 tablespoons Hungarian paprika or 3 tablespoons paprika plus ¼ teaspoon cayenne pepper
1 teaspoon salt

½ teaspoon pepper
2 tomatoes, peeled, chopped
2½ cups water

* * * * *

1 large green pepper or ½ red pepper and ½ green pepper, cut into chunks

* * * * *

Cooked egg noodles, optional

✽ Low Calorie
Servings: 6
Per Serving
Calories: 170
Fat: 10.4 g
Sodium: 391 mg
Cholesterol: 38 mg

(Shown on page 159)

Heat oil in pressure cooker over medium heat. Brown short ribs, a few at a time and remove. Add onions and more oil, if needed, to pressure cooker. Sauté until tender. Stir in paprika, salt, and pepper. Stir in tomatoes and water. Return short ribs to pressure cooker. Close cover securely. Place pressure regulator on vent pipe. COOK 22 MINUTES at 15 pounds pressure. Quick cool cooker. Stir in green pepper. Close cover securely. Place pressure regulator on vent pipe. COOK 3 MINUTES at 15 pounds pressure. Let pressure drop of its own accord. Serve with noodles.

● ● ● ● ● ● ●

Pesto Beef Roast

2 tablespoons olive oil
1 (3- to 3½-pound) boneless beef rump roast, trimmed
½ cup fresh or frozen (thawed) pesto
¾ cup beef stock or broth
¾ cup dry red wine

1 cup water

* * * * *

Salt
Pepper
12 ounces fettucine, cooked, drained
Grated Parmesan cheese

Servings: 8
Per Serving
Calories: 501
Fat: 20.2 g
Sodium: 207 mg
Cholesterol: 154 mg

Heat oil in pressure cooker over medium heat. Brown roast on all sides. Remove roast and cool slightly. Make several deep slits in top surface of roast. Fill slits with pesto. Place cooking rack (or basket), beef stock, wine, and water in pressure cooker. Place roast on rack (or in basket). Close cover securely. Place pressure regulator on vent pipe. COOK 35 MINUTES at 15 pounds pressure. Let pressure drop of its own accord. Remove roast and rack (or basket) from pressure cooker. Season to taste with salt and pepper. Keep warm. Boil pan juices to reduce by half. Toss fettucine with pan juices. Sprinkle with cheese. Serve with roast.

Intro

Basics

Appetizers

Soups and Stocks

Meats

Poultry

Seafood

Vegetables

Breads

Desserts

Whole Meal Magic

5.

Mahogany-Sauced Lamb Shanks

2 tablespoons vegetable oil
1 (3- to 4-pound) cross-cut lamb shank
2 cups hot water
¼ cup soy sauce
3 tablespoons rice wine or dry sherry
¼ lemon, thinly sliced

1 teaspoon sugar
3 thin slices fresh ginger or ¼ teaspoon ground ginger
¼ teaspoon anise seeds

＊ ＊ ＊ ＊ ＊

2 tablespoons cornstarch
2 tablespoons cold water
Hot cooked noodles

Servings: 6
Per Serving
Calories: 316
Fat: 14.5 g
Sodium: 774 mg
Cholesterol: 115 mg

(Shown on page 148)

Heat oil in 6- or 8-quart pressure cooker over medium heat. Brown lamb shanks and remove. Add hot water to pressure cooker. Stir in soy sauce, wine, lemon, sugar, ginger, and anise seeds. Return shanks to pressure cooker. Close cover securely. Place pressure regulator on vent pipe. COOK 30 MINUTES at 15 pounds pressure. Quick cool cooker. Remove shanks from pressure cooker. Keep warm. Skim fat from cooking liquid. Mix cornstarch with cold water. Stir into cooking liquid. Cook and stir until sauce boils and thickens. Serve with lamb shanks and noodles.

● ● ● ● ● ● ●

Servings: 8
Per Serving
Calories: 332
Fat: 12.8 g
Sodium: 932 mg
Cholesterol: 77 mg

(Shown on page 62)

Apricot Barbecue Pork Roast

3 pound boneless rolled pork roast
½ cup catsup
½ cup apricot preserves
¼ cup packed dark brown sugar
¼ cup cider vinegar

½ cup teriyaki sauce
1 teaspoon crushed red pepper
1 teaspoon dry mustard
¼ teaspoon ground pepper
1 large onion, sliced
3 cups water

Place pork roast in a large plastic bag or glass dish. Combine catsup, preserves, brown sugar, vinegar, teriyaki sauce, red pepper, mustard, and pepper. Mix thoroughly and pour over pork. Refrigerate overnight. Remove pork; reserve marinade. Brown pork on all sides in pressure cooker over medium heat; remove. Place cooking rack (or basket), half of sliced onion, and water in pressure cooker. Place pork roast on rack (or in basket) and arrange remaining onion evenly on top of roast. Close cover securely. Place pressure regulator on vent pipe. COOK 60 MINUTES at 15 pounds pressure. Let pressure drop of its own accord. Place reserved marinade in saucepan and simmer until thickened, stirring occasionally. Remove roast and onions from pressure cooker. Add onions to thickened marinade and serve with sliced pork. Onions may be puréed before adding to sauce and served with rice, if desired.

Moroccan Lamb Stew

❋ *Low Calorie*
Servings: 8
Per Serving
Calories: 226
Fat: 10.6 g
Sodium: 194 mg
Cholesterol: 137 mg

1 tablespoon vegetable oil
2 pounds lean boneless lamb, cut into ¾-inch cubes
1½ cups chopped onions
1 teaspoon minced fresh ginger
1 large clove garlic, minced
1 bay leaf
¼ teaspoon crushed saffron threads or ground turmeric
Generous pinch ground cloves

1½ cups water
1 cup tomato purée
　　　* * * * *
Salt
Pepper
¼ cup dark raisins
¼ cup toasted blanched almonds
3 hard-cooked eggs, cut into quarters
Hot cooked rice

Heat oil in pressure cooker over medium heat. Brown lamb on all sides. Remove lamb and reserve. Add onions, ginger, and garlic to pressure cooker. Sauté until tender. Stir in bay leaf, saffron, cloves, water, tomato purée, and reserved lamb. Close cover securely. Place pressure regulator on vent pipe. COOK 12 MINUTES at 15 pounds pressure. Let pressure drop of its own accord. Season to taste with salt and pepper. Sprinkle stew with raisins and almonds. Garnish with eggs. Serve with rice.

Osso Buco (Braised Veal Shanks)

Servings: 4
Per Serving
Calories: 350
Fat: 12.2 g
Sodium: 148 mg
Cholesterol: 159 mg

1 tablespoon olive or vegetable oil
4 veal shanks (about 2¼ pounds)
½ cup sliced onion
2 cloves garlic, minced
1 teaspoon dried basil
½ teaspoon dried thyme
1 bay leaf

2 medium tomatoes, chopped
1 cup dry white wine
1 small carrot, chopped
　　　* * * * *
2 tablespoons minced parsley
1 tablespoon grated lemon rind
Salt
Pepper

Heat oil in 6- or 8-quart pressure cooker over medium heat. Brown veal shanks; remove and reserve. Add onion and garlic to pressure cooker. Sauté 1 minute. Stir in basil, thyme, bay leaf, tomatoes, wine, and carrot. Return veal shanks to pressure cooker. Close cover securely. Place pressure regulator on vent pipe. COOK 12 MINUTES at 15 pounds pressure. Let pressure drop of its own accord. Stir in parsley and lemon rind. Season to taste with salt and pepper.

Intro

Basics

Appetizers

Soups and Stocks

Meats

Poultry

Seafood

Vegetables

Breads

Desserts

Whole Meal Magic

Rabbit with Prunes

1 tablespoon olive or vegetable oil	2 cups pitted prunes
1¾ pound rabbit, cut into quarters	* * * * *
1 cup chopped onion	1 tablespoon tomato paste
1 cup finely chopped carrot	1 tablespoon all-purpose flour
2 cloves garlic, minced	½ cup dry red wine or chicken stock or broth
¼ teaspoon dried thyme	Salt
¼ teaspoon dried marjoram	Pepper
1½ cups dry red wine or chicken stock or broth	

❤ *Low Cholesterol*

Servings: 4
Per Serving
Calories: 479
Fat: 9.4 g
Sodium: 76 mg
Cholesterol: 56 mg

Heat oil in 6- or 8-quart pressure cooker over medium heat. Brown rabbit on all sides. Remove rabbit and reserve. Add onion, carrot, and garlic; sauté until tender. Stir in thyme, marjoram, wine, and prunes. Return rabbit to pressure cooker. Close cover securely. Place pressure regulator on vent pipe. COOK 6 MINUTES at 15 pounds pressure. Let pressure drop of its own accord. Combine tomato paste, flour, wine, salt, and pepper. Pour into pressure cooker and simmer to desired thickness.

● ● ● ● ● ● ●

Servings: 8
Per Serving
Calories: 367
Fat: 12.8 g
Sodium: 895 mg
Cholesterol: 126 mg

Quick Sauerbraten

2 tablespoons vegetable oil	1 teaspoon dried thyme
3½ pound chuck roast	3 onions, sliced
2 cups vinegar	1 clove garlic, halved
2 cups water	1 tablespoon ground cloves
1 tablespoon salt	3 bay leaves
½ teaspoon pepper	5 celery tops
3 tablespoons brown sugar	6 finely ground ginger snaps, optional
½ teaspoon sage	

Heat oil in pressure cooker over medium heat. Brown roast on all sides. Add remaining ingredients. Close cover securely. Place pressure regulator on vent pipe. COOK 35 MINUTES at 15 pounds pressure. Let pressure drop of its own accord.

Spicy Sausage, Red Beans and Rice

1 tablespoon vegetable oil
⅓ cup chopped onion
⅓ cup chopped green pepper
½ jalapeño pepper, seeds and veins discarded, minced
1 (15½-ounce) can red beans, drained
12 ounces cooked smoked sausage, cut into ½-inch pieces
1 cup water

1 cup chicken stock
1 teaspoon cider vinegar
1 teaspoon red pepper sauce
1 teaspoon dried oregano
1 teaspoon dried thyme
½ teaspoon crushed red pepper

* * * * *

1 cup cooked rice
1 teaspoon sugar

Servings: 4
Per Serving
Calories: 526
Fat: 30.9 g
Sodium: 1646 mg
Cholesterol: 71 mg

Heat oil in pressure cooker over medium heat. Sauté onion and pepper until tender. Add remaining ingredients, except rice and sugar. Close cover securely. Place pressure regulator on vent pipe. COOK 4 MINUTES at 15 pounds pressure. Let pressure drop of its own accord. Stir in rice and sugar.

• • • • • • •

Pork Chops for Two

1 tablespoon olive or vegetable oil
2 pork chops, cut ¾ inch thick
¼ cup dry white wine
1½ cups water
½ teaspoon salt

Dash each: dried oregano, thyme, and marjoram
1 small onion, cut in half
2 small to medium artichokes, washed and trimmed

Servings: 2
Per Serving
Calories: 324
Fat: 17.1 g
Sodium: 699 mg
Cholesterol: 63 mg

(Shown on page 158)

Heat oil in 6- or 8-quart pressure cooker over medium heat; brown chops on both sides and remove from pan. Add wine, water, salt, and herbs, stirring to deglaze pan. Dip-cut surface of artichoke into wine mixture. Return pork chops to pan with onion. Place rack (or basket) over chops and arrange artichokes on rack (or in basket). Close cover securely. Place pressure regulator on vent pipe. COOK 15 MINUTES at 15 pounds pressure. Quick cool cooker.

Intro

Basics

Appetizers

Soups and Stocks

Meats

Poultry

Seafood

Vegetables

Breads

Desserts

Whole Meal Magic

5.

Presto Spareribs

3 pounds spareribs, cut into serving pieces
1 tablespoon dry mustard
1 tablespoon chili powder
½ teaspoon cayenne pepper
1 clove garlic
2 tablespoons vegetable oil
2 cups water
⅔ cup catsup
½ cup chopped onion
¼ cup light molasses
¼ cup lemon juice
1 teaspoon oregano
½ teaspoon salt
¼ teaspoon freshly ground pepper
2 drops liquid smoke

Servings: 6
Per Serving
Calories: 491
Fat: 27.4 g
Sodium: 460 mg
Cholesterol: 134 mg

Trim excess fat from ribs. Combine dry mustard, chili powder, and cayenne pepper. Sprinkle over ribs. Rub seasoning into ribs using cut surface of garlic clove. Heat oil in pressure cooker over medium heat. Brown ribs and remove. Pour off excess fat. Place water and cooking rack (or basket) in pressure cooker. Combine remaining ingredients. Spread mixture on meaty side of ribs. Place ribs on rack (or in basket). Close cover securely. Place pressure regulator on vent pipe. COOK 15 MINUTES at 15 pounds pressure. Quick cool cooker. If crisping is desired, place ribs under broiler 1 to 3 minutes.

Spiced Brisket

Servings: 8
Per Serving
Calories: 336
Fat: 16.2 g
Sodium: 159 mg
Cholesterol: 117 mg

3 pound beef brisket
¼ teaspoon salt
¼ teaspoon coarse ground pepper
⅛ teaspoon nutmeg
⅛ teaspoon cloves
⅛ teaspoon garlic powder
¼ cup molasses
1 medium onion, sliced
2 bay leaves (crumbled)
2½ cups water

Trim fat from brisket. Cut brisket in half crosswise. Stir salt, pepper, nutmeg, cloves, and garlic powder into molasses. Brush all sides of meat with mixture. Lay onion slices and bay leaves on top of one piece of meat. Tie two pieces of meat tightly together with string. Cover and let set at room temperature for one hour. Place water and cooking rack (or basket) in 6- or 8-quart pressure cooker. Place meat on rack (or in basket). Close cover securely. Place pressure regulator on vent pipe. COOK 40 MINUTES at 15 pounds pressure. Let pressure drop of its own accord. Remove meat from pressure cooker and slice across grain.

Smothered Steak

Servings: 6
Per Serving
Calories: 409
Fat: 12.3 g
Sodium: 551 mg
Cholesterol: 96 mg

2 pounds boneless beef round steak, 1½ to 2 inches thick, trimmed
2 tablespoons vegetable oil
1 (10-ounce) can condensed beef broth
1¼ cups water
1 medium onion, sliced
1 tablespoon fresh or 1 teaspoon dried sage, thyme, basil, or rosemary
1 clove garlic, minced

* * * * *

6 medium white potatoes

* * * *

2 tablespoons all-purpose flour
¼ cup cold water
Salt
Pepper

Cut steak into 6 even-sized pieces. Heat oil in pressure cooker over medium heat. Brown steak. Add beef broth, 1¼ cups water, onion, sage, and garlic. Close cover securely. Place pressure regulator on vent pipe. COOK 10 MINUTES at 15 pounds pressure. Quick cool cooker. Place cooking rack (or basket) on top of steak in pressure cooker. Place potatoes on rack (or in basket). Close cover securely. Place pressure regulator on vent pipe. COOK 10 MINUTES at 15 pounds pressure. Let pressure drop of its own accord. Remove potatoes, rack (or basket), and steak. Keep warm. Mix 2 tablespoons flour with ¼ cup water. Stir into broth in pressure cooker. Cook and stir until sauce boils and thickens. Season to taste with salt and pepper. Serve sauce with steak.

● ● ● ● ● ● ●

Pot Roast Royale

Servings: 8
Per Serving
Calories: 337
Fat: 18.8 g
Sodium: 403 mg
Cholesterol: 115 mg

(Shown on page 145)

1 tablespoon vegetable oil
3 pound beef brisket or boneless chuck roast
1 onion, thinly sliced
1 (2-ounce) can anchovy fillets, drained and chopped
1 bay leaf
9 peppercorns
1 tablespoon packed brown sugar
1 tablespoon cider vinegar
2½ cups water

Heat oil in pressure cooker over medium heat. Lightly brown roast on all sides. Remove from cooker. Add onion to cooker and cook until lightly browned. Remove from cooker. Combine anchovies, bay leaf, peppercorns, sugar, vinegar, and water in pressure cooker. Place cooking rack (or basket) and roast in cooker. Arrange onions evenly on top of roast. Close cover securely. Place pressure regulator on vent pipe. COOK 45 MINUTES at 15 pounds pressure. Let pressure drop of its own accord. Remove roast and onion; keep warm. If desired, thicken cooking liquid to make gravy or serve roast with horseradish.

Intro

Basics

Appetizers

Soups and Stocks

Meats

Poultry

Seafood

Vegetables

Breads

Desserts

Whole Meal Magic

5.

Swiss Steak Presto

2 pounds boneless beef round steak, 1½ to 2 inches thick, trimmed
2 tablespoons all-purpose flour
½ teaspoon salt
½ teaspoon dried basil
¼ teaspoon pepper
¼ teaspoon garlic powder
⅛ teaspoon ground allspice
2 tablespoons vegetable oil
8 small pearl onions

1 green pepper, cut into 8 chunks
2 large red-skinned potatoes, pared, cut into quarters
1 (16-ounce) can whole tomatoes, undrained
1½ cups water

* * * * *

¼ cup cornstarch
¼ cup cold water

Servings: 6
Per Serving
Calories: 347
Fat: 11.9 g
Sodium: 374 mg
Cholesterol: 96 mg

Cut steak into 6 even-sized pieces. Mix flour, salt, basil, pepper, garlic powder, and allspice. Sprinkle over steak. Using large knife, pound seasoned flour into both sides of steak until all flour is used. Heat oil in 6- or 8-quart pressure cooker over medium heat. Sauté onions and green pepper 3 minutes. Remove vegetables and reserve. Brown steak on both sides and remove. Place cooking rack (or basket), steak, and reserved vegetables in pressure cooker. Add potatoes, tomatoes, and 1½ cups water. Close cover securely. Place pressure regulator on vent pipe. COOK 15 MINUTES at 15 pounds pressure. Let pressure drop of its own accord. Remove steak and vegetables. Keep warm. Mix cornstarch with ¼ cup water. Stir into cooking liquid in pressure cooker. Cook and stir until sauce boils and thickens. Serve sauce over steak and vegetables.

Orange Sauced Pork Roast

❋ *Low Calorie*
Servings: 8
Per Serving
Calories: 270
Fat: 15.1 g
Sodium: 222 mg
Cholesterol: 77 mg

3 pound semi-boneless pork loin roast (rib removed)
20 slivers garlic
2 tablespoons cooking oil
1 (13¾-ounce) can chicken broth
1½ cups water
¼ teaspoon crushed red pepper
⅓ cup chopped cilantro (Chinese parsley or fresh coriander)
4 bay leaves
4 whole allspice

* * * * *

Orange Sauce (recipe follows)

Remove excess fat from roast. Trim to fit in a 6- or 8-quart pressure cooker, if necessary. Make slits in pork roast and insert garlic slivers. Heat oil in pressure cooker over medium heat. Brown meat on all sides in hot oil. Add chicken broth, water, red pepper, cilantro, bay leaves, and allspice. Close cover securely. Place pressure regulator on vent pipe. COOK 60 MINUTES at 15 pounds pressure. Let pressure drop of its own accord. Remove meat. Strain broth and reserve.

Orange Sauce

1 teaspoon butter or margarine
6 green onions, sliced
2 tablespoons flour
¼ teaspoon dry mustard
1 cup reserved broth from roast
½ cup orange juice
1 tablespoon lime or lemon juice
Salt
Cilantro, chopped

Heat butter in pressure cooker over medium heat; add green onions and cook until tender. Stir in flour and mustard; add 1 cup reserved broth, orange, and lime juice. Cook and stir until thickened. Season with salt and chopped cilantro. Serve with roast pork.

Intro

Basics

Appetizers

Soups and Stocks

Meats

Poultry

Seafood

Vegetables

Breads

Desserts

Whole Meal Magic

5. Chilorio
(Mexican pork filling for Burritos or Tacos)

1 (2½- to 3-pound) pork
   shoulder or loin roast
   Salt
   Pepper
1 medium onion, sliced
3 cups water

* * * * *

2 medium green peppers,
   seeded and cut up
2 large cloves garlic
¼ teaspoon cumin seeds
½ teaspoon oregano

½ teaspoon ground black pepper

* * * * *

¼ cup lemon juice or white
   vinegar
½ teaspoon salt
⅛ teaspoon cayenne pepper
2 tablespoons chopped cilantro
   or parsley
10 (10-inch) flour tortillas or 24
   taco shells
   Lettuce, tomato, cheese, sour
   cream

✿ **Low Calorie**

Servings: 10 Burritos
Per Serving
Calories: 339
Fat: 14.3 g
Sodium: 166 mg
Cholesterol: 74 mg

(Shown on page 53)

Servings: 24 Tacos
Per Serving
Calories: 132
Fat: 7 g
Sodium: 69 mg
Cholesterol: 31 mg

Trim as much surface fat from meat as possible. Sprinkle both sides with salt and pepper. Put rack (or basket), meat, sliced onion, and water in 6- or 8-quart pressure cooker. Close cover securely. Place pressure regulator on vent pipe. COOK 60 MINUTES at 15 pounds pressure. Let pressure drop of its own accord. Remove meat and rack (or basket). Boil juices rapidly to reduce to 1 cup. Add green peppers, garlic, cumin seeds, oregano, and black pepper. Close cover securely. Place pressure regulator on vent pipe. COOK 2 MINUTES at 15 pounds pressure. Quick cool cooker. Purée mixture in blender or food processor; add lemon juice and salt. You should have about 2 cups green sauce mixture. Remove meat from bones, discarding them and any fat. Chop meat with a knife or in a food processor using an on-and-off action. You should have about 3 cups. Add half the green sauce to meat, mixing well. Add cayenne and cilantro to remaining sauce.

To make Burritos: Warm tortillas quickly in a hot fry pan. (Tortillas may be heated in a microwave oven. Wrap 2 at a time in plastic wrap and microwave on high for 30 seconds.) Spread about 1 tablespoon of green sauce on each tortilla. Place ⅓ cup of meat mixture to one side of center, spreading slightly. Wrap meat in tortilla by folding in ends and rolling. May be served soft or fried. Accompany with sour cream, if desired.

To make Tacos: Heat taco shells. Place about 2 tablespoons of meat mixture in each shell; top with lettuce, tomato, cheese, sour cream, and additional sauce.

Shrimp-Stuffed Steak Roll

Servings: 6
Per Serving
Calories: 439
Fat: 22.7 g
Sodium: 444 mg
Cholesterol: 152 mg

1½ pound flank steak or top round steak, about ½ inch thick
2 tablespoons lemon juice
2 tablespoons vegetable oil
Salt
Pepper
1 (7-ounce) can tiny shrimp, drained
¼ cup fresh bread crumbs
1 tablespoon minced green onion
1 small clove garlic, minced

½ teaspoon dried basil
¼ teaspoon red pepper sauce
3 Romaine lettuce leaves, spines removed, or 8 to 10 spinach or sorrel leaves
1 tablespoon vegetable oil
2 cups water
½ cup dry red wine

* * * * *

2 (5-ounce) packages frozen prepared chicken a la king or creamed chipped beef
Hot cooked rice

Butterfly steak and pound lightly to even out thickness. Mix lemon juice and 2 tablespoons oil. Brush half the lemon-oil on steak. Sprinkle with salt and pepper. Let stand at room temperature. Combine remaining lemon-oil, shrimp, bread crumbs, green onion, garlic, basil, and pepper sauce. Soften lettuce leaves under hot tap water. Pat dry. Place on top of steak. Spread shrimp stuffing on top of lettuce. Roll up steak and tie securely in several places. Heat 1 tablespoon oil in 6- or 8-quart pressure cooker over medium heat. Brown steak roll on all sides, curving to fit in pressure cooker. Add water and wine. Close cover securely. Place pressure regulator on vent pipe. COOK 20 MINUTES at 15 pounds pressure. Let pressure drop of its own accord. Remove steak roll. Keep warm. Boil cooking liquid until reduced to ¾ cup. Add chicken a la king. Cook and stir until hot. Serve as sauce over rice and sliced steak roll.

5. Soft Tacos Picadillo

2½	cups water		Pinch ground cloves
1½	pound beef skirt steak or flank steak	1½	cups chopped tomatoes
		¼	cup toasted slivered almonds
	* * * * *	¼	cup dark raisins
2	tablespoons vegetable oil		Salt
1	cup chopped onion	16	flour tortillas, heated
2	cloves garlic, minced		Guacamole
1	small jalapeño chile, seeded, deveined, minced		Sour cream or sour half-and-half
1-1½	teaspoons ground cinnamon		Hot or mild salsa
½	teaspoon dried oregano		

Servings: 8
Per Serving
Calories: 445
Fat: 17.6 g
Sodium: 74 mg
Cholesterol: 57 mg

Place cooking rack (or basket) and 2½ cups water in pressure cooker. Place steak on rack (or in basket). Close cover securely. Place pressure regulator on vent pipe. COOK 35 MINUTES at 15 pounds pressure. Let pressure drop of its own accord. Remove steak and cool. Discard liquid. Shred steak with fork into bite-size pieces. Heat oil in pressure cooker over medium heat. Sauté beef until browned and beginning to crisp. Remove beef and reserve. Add onion, garlic, chile, cinnamon, oregano, and cloves to pressure cooker. Sauté until onion is tender. Stir in reserved beef, tomatoes, almonds, and raisins; heat until hot. Season to taste with salt. Spoon about ¼ cup beef mixture into center of a tortilla, top with guacamole, sour cream, and salsa to taste, and roll up. Makes 8 servings, 2 tortillas each.

Mustard Pecan Tenderloin

1 pork tenderloin, about 1 pound
1 tablespoon olive oil
¼ cup Dijon mustard
1 clove garlic, minced
1 tablespoon honey
1 tablespoon molasses
1 teaspoon grated orange peel
2 tablespoons fresh bread crumbs

2 tablespoons finely chopped toasted pecans
Juice of 1 orange plus water to make 2 cups

* * * * *

2 sweet potatoes, about 1 pound

* * * * *

1 pound fresh asparagus spears, cooked

Servings: 4
Per Serving
Calories: 429
Fat: 12.7 g
Sodium: 318 mg
Cholesterol: 105 mg

Remove excess fat from tenderloin, if necessary. Cut into 4 or 5 equal pieces. Brown tenderloin in olive oil in 6- or 8-quart pressure cooker over medium heat. Remove from pan and cool slightly. Combine mustard, garlic, honey, molasses, orange peel, and bread crumbs. Spread on top and sides of tenderloin, using about half, sprinkle with pecans. Let stand for 30 minutes. Put orange juice and water in pressure cooker. Place rack (or basket) in cooker. Arrange tenderloin on rack (or in basket). Close cover securely. Place pressure regulator on vent pipe. COOK 10 MINUTES at 15 pounds pressure. Quick cool cooker. Remove tenderloin and rack (or basket). Pare and slice sweet potatoes and place in pressure cooker. Close cover securely. Place pressure regulator on vent pipe. COOK 5 MINUTES at 15 pounds pressure. Quick cool cooker. Add remaining mustard mixture to broth in pan with sweet potatoes. Serve with cooked asparagus.

Intro

Basics

Appetizers

Soups and Stocks

Meats

Poultry

Seafood

Vegetables

Breads

Desserts

Whole Meal Magic

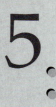

5. *Sweet-and-Sour Spareribs, Chinese Style*

3 pounds spareribs, cut into serving pieces
Salt
Pepper
1 tablespoon vegetable oil

1½ cups water
⅓ cup soy sauce
3 tablespoons sherry
1 teaspoon sugar
¼ teaspoon ground ginger

Sauce

3 tablespoons vinegar
3 tablespoons sugar

2 tablespoons cornstarch
½ cup water

✿ *Low Calorie*
Servings: 6
Per Serving
Calories: 211
Fat: 12.4 g
Sodium: 936 mg
Cholesterol: 38 mg

Season ribs with salt and pepper. Heat oil in pressure cooker over medium heat. Brown ribs on all sides. Add water, soy sauce, sherry, sugar, and ginger. Close cover securely. Place pressure regulator on vent pipe. COOK 15 MINUTES at 15 pounds pressure. Let pressure drop of its own accord. Remove spareribs to a warm platter. Prepare sauce. Blend vinegar, sugar, and cornstarch into water; stir into hot liquid. Cook and stir until mixture boils and thickens. Pour sauce over ribs.

Texas Barbecued Pot Roast

Servings: 6
Per Serving
Calories: 472
Fat: 10.8 g
Sodium: 749 mg
Cholesterol: 144 mg

½	cup catsup	¼	teaspoon black pepper
½	cup teriyaki or soy sauce	1	(3- to 3½-pound) beef eye of
½	cup apricot preserves		round, bottom round,
¼	cup packed dark brown sugar		boneless chuck roast or
¼	cup distilled white vinegar		pork loin roast
1	teaspoon crushed red pepper	2½	cups water
1	teaspoon dry mustard	1	large onion, sliced

Mix catsup, teriyaki sauce, preserves, brown sugar, vinegar, red pepper, mustard, and black pepper. Place roast and barbecue sauce in plastic bag or glass dish. Close bag securely or cover dish. Marinate in refrigerator overnight. Remove roast from sauce, reserving sauce. Place cooking rack (or basket) and water in 6- or 8-quart pressure cooker. Cover rack (or basket) with half the onion. Place roast on onion. Cover with remaining onion. Close cover securely. Place pressure regulator on vent pipe. Cook at 15 pounds pressure, for following degrees of doneness: COOK BEEF 8-10 MINUTES **per pound** for rare; 10-12 MINUTES **per pound** for medium; AT LEAST 12-15 MINUTES **per pound** for well-done. COOK PORK 15 MINUTES **per pound** for well-done. Let pressure drop of its own accord. Meanwhile, in a saucepan, heat reserved sauce to a gentle boil, stirring constantly until reduced by about half. Remove roast from pressure cooker. Keep warm. Discard cooking water. Purée onion in blender or food processor. Add to reduced sauce. Serve sauce with sliced beef.

5. *Kibbe*

½ cup bulgur (cracked wheat)
½ cup warm water
1 pound ground lean lamb or beef
¼ cup pine nuts or slivered almonds
¼ cup finely chopped onion
1½ teaspoons garlic powder
1 teaspoon salt
½ teaspoon ground allspice
¼ teaspoon ground cinnamon

¼ teaspoon pepper
2 tablespoons olive or vegetable oil
1½ cups water

½ cup plain non-fat yogurt
½ cup finely chopped seeded cucumber
¼ cup finely chopped onion
½ teaspoon garlic salt
½ teaspoon dried mint

Servings: 4
Per Serving
Calories: 316
Fat: 16.7 g
Sodium: 859 mg
Cholesterol: 58 mg

Mix bulgur and ½ cup warm water. Let stand until water is absorbed. Mix bulgur, lamb, pine nuts, ¼ cup onion, garlic powder, salt, allspice, cinnamon, and pepper. Shape into 24 meatballs. Heat oil in pressure cooker over medium heat. Brown meatballs on all sides. Remove meatballs and drain on paper towels. Place cooking rack (or basket) and 1½ cups water in pressure cooker. Place 12 meatballs on rack (or in basket). Close cover securely. Place pressure regulator on vent pipe. COOK 3 MINUTES at 15 pounds pressure. Quick cool cooker. Mix yogurt and remaining ingredients. Serve with meatballs.

Beef & Tomato Spaghetti Sauce

Servings: 6
Per Serving
Calories: 416
Fat: 20.8 g
Sodium: 823 mg
Cholesterol: 51 mg

¼ cup olive oil
2 carrots, finely chopped
1 cup chopped celery
2 medium yellow onions, peeled and finely chopped
1 pound ground beef
1 (28-ounce) can plum tomatoes, drained
1½ cups red wine
2 cloves garlic, peeled and chopped

½ cup mushrooms
⅓ cup grated Parmesan cheese
2 teaspoons basil
2 tablespoons oregano
2 tablespoons sugar
Salt
Pepper

* * * * *

2 (6-ounce) cans tomato paste
⅓ cup chopped parsley
Hot spaghetti

Heat oil in 6- or 8-quart pressure cooker over medium heat. Sauté carrots, celery, and onions until tender. Add beef and brown. Stir in tomatoes, wine, garlic, mushrooms, cheese, basil, oregano, sugar, salt, and pepper. Close cover securely. Place pressure regulator on vent pipe. COOK 8 MINUTES at 15 pounds pressure. Let pressure drop of its own accord. Stir in tomato paste and parsley. Simmer to desired thickness. Serve over hot spaghetti.

Intro

Basics

Appetizers

Soups and Stocks

Meats

Poultry

Seafood

Vegetables

Breads

Desserts

Whole Meal Magic

Notes

6. Poultry

> **"**...a growing appreciation for chicken's lower fat, lower cholesterol...**"**

When Herbert Hoover won election to the presidency in November 1928 with the slogan, "A chicken in every pot!," little did he know how hard it would be to keep that promise. The Great Depression hit in 1929, and chicken became a very scarce commodity. Cash-strapped home-makers compensated with creative menus planned around fish, veal, and pork! There even was a popular recipe entitled "City Chicken" that was a combination of seasoned pork and veal cubes served on a skewer to resemble drumsticks!

Such kitchen improvisation reemerged in the mid-forties when the war, not prices, made many foods, including chicken, hard to come by. When the war was over, however, consumers were rewarded with an unprecedented abundance and variety of foods.

New supermarkets with expanded services offered cut-up chickens with the most desirable cuts packaged together. Cooks no longer had to buy four or more chickens to serve one dinner of chicken breasts to their guests. That made their families happy too, because it meant they didn't have to dine on the leftover backs and wings for days!

6.

Time and money were no problem in the easy-going fifties, so kitchen ingenuity was more of an opportunity than a necessity. That certainly didn't deter many home chefs from getting creative with chicken—now a thriftier alternative to meat. Traditional fried chicken was the hands down favorite for picnics, potluck suppers, and tailgate parties, however, when it came to serious entertaining, hostesses proudly presented Coq Au Vin, Chicken Kiev, or Chicken Divan.

Foreign cookery, in fact, did wonders for the image of chicken over the next few decades. Hand in hand with a growing appreciation for chicken's lower-fat, lower-cholesterol advantages, and the abundance of ethnic chicken dishes made poultry the number one protein choice in restaurants and at the family dinner table. Stir-fried Chinese Almond Chicken, Chicken Fajitas, and Chicken Curry became new menu standards.

It probably won't surprise you that the pressure cooker is a perfect culinary match for poultry in any of its creative forms and disguises. Not only does pressure cooking capitalize on poultry's popularity and economy, it multiplies the healthy assets of poultry as well.

Since poultry skin does not crisp and brown in the pressure cooker, removing the skin before cooking lowers the fat considerably without detracting from the appearance or appeal of the final product. As a matter of fact, the result is chicken meat that is remarkably moist, incredibly tender, and deliciously infused with all the marvelous flavors of its cooking sauce.

With the pressure cooker, you're only minutes away from savory chicken stew, herbed chicken breasts, and even chicken pot pie! For this chapter, we've compiled an assortment of poultry recipes—from the traditional to the trendy, from the classy to the casual—to show-off the pressure cooker's versatility and speed. We've included international favorites, such as *Chicken Paprika* and *Sweet 'n Sour Chicken*, and some new-age inspired innovations like *California Chicken & Artichokes* and *Chicken Couscous with Raspberry Vinegar*.

San Francisco Chicken

1 (3- to 3½-pound) chicken,
   cut up
1 large green pepper, cut into
   thin strips
1 large onion, cut into thin
   strips
1 teaspoon grated orange rind
2½ cups water

* * * * *

¾ cup orange juice

¼ cup dry sherry
¼ cup soy sauce
2 tablespoons packed brown
   sugar
2 tablespoons cornstarch
1 tablespoon butter or
   margarine
¼ teaspoon ground ginger
½ cup slivered almonds

❀ *Low Calorie*
Servings: 6
Per Serving
Calories: 161
Fat: 8 g
Sodium: 204 mg
Cholesterol: 48 mg

(Shown on page 151)

Place chicken pieces on large piece of aluminum foil. Cover with green pepper, onion, and orange rind. Wrap securely in foil. Place cooking rack (or basket) and water in 6- or 8-quart pressure cooker. Place chicken packet on rack (or in basket). Close cover securely. Place pressure regulator on vent pipe. COOK 20 MINUTES at 15 pounds pressure. Let pressure drop of its own accord. Remove chicken, vegetables, and liquid from cooker. Mix remaining ingredients except almonds in saucepan. Cook and stir until sauce boils and thickens. Unwrap chicken and vegetables. Top with orange sauce and almonds.

● ● ● ● ● ● ●

Cornish Hens with Burgundy Cherry Sauce

2 Cornish hens
  Salt
  Pepper
2 tablespoons vegetable oil
1 cup red burgundy wine
½ cup water
4 cloves garlic, chopped

1½ cups canned dark sweet
    pitted cherries
3 tablespoons sugar

* * * * *

2 teaspoons cornstarch
2 tablespoons water

Servings: 4
Per Serving
Calories: 101
Fat: 49.2 g
Sodium: 185 mg
Cholesterol: 373 mg

Season Cornish hens with salt and pepper. Heat oil in 6- or 8-quart pressure cooker over medium heat. Brown Cornish hens. Add wine, water, garlic, cherries, and sugar. Close cover securely. Place pressure regulator on vent pipe. COOK 8 MINUTES at 15 pounds pressure. Let pressure drop of its own accord. Remove Cornish hens to a warm platter. Blend cornstarch into water; stir into hot liquid. Cook and stir until mixture thickens. Serve sauce with Cornish hens.

Intro

Basics

Appetizers

Soups
and
Stocks

Meats

Poultry

Seafood

Vegetables

Breads

Desserts

Whole
Meal
Magic

93

Bayou Bounty Chicken

2 tablespoons vegetable oil
1 (3- to 3½-pound) chicken, cut up
1 (28-ounce) can whole tomatoes, undrained, cut up
½ cup water
2 onions, chopped
1 green pepper, seeded, chopped

1 cup chopped celery
1 tablespoon extra spicy seasoning blend
2 cloves garlic, minced

* * * * *

Hot cooked rice

Servings: 6
Per Serving
Calories: 341
Fat: 17.6 g
Sodium: 288 mg
Cholesterol: 93 mg

Heat oil in 6- or 8-quart pressure cooker over medium heat. Brown chicken, a few pieces at a time, and remove. Add remaining ingredients except rice to pressure cooker. Return chicken to pressure cooker. Close cover securely. Place pressure regulator on vent pipe. COOK 8 MINUTES at 15 pounds pressure. Let pressure drop of its own accord. Remove chicken. Simmer sauce to thicken. Serve chicken and sauce over rice.

Servings: 6
Per Serving
Calories: 387
Fat: 24.6 g
Sodium: 319 mg
Cholesterol: 121 mg

Chicken Paprika

1 (3- to 3½-pound) chicken, cut up
Salt
Pepper
3-4 tablespoons butter or margarine
1 medium onion, chopped
1 medium green pepper, chopped
5 cloves garlic, minced

¼ cup tomato sauce
3 tablespoons dillweed
2 tablespoons Hungarian paprika
1 cup chicken stock or broth
½ cup water

* * * * *

1 tablespoon all-purpose flour
¾ cup sour cream

Sprinkle chicken with salt and pepper. Heat butter in pressure cooker over medium heat. Sauté onion, green pepper, and garlic until tender and remove. Brown chicken, a few pieces at a time, and remove. Add tomato sauce, dillweed, paprika, and a small amount of chicken stock to pressure cooker. Mix well. Stir in remaining stock and water. Return chicken and vegetables to pressure cooker. Close cover securely. Place pressure regulator on vent pipe. COOK 8 MINUTES at 15 pounds pressure. Let pressure drop of its own accord. Remove chicken and vegetables. Keep warm. Mix flour with sour cream. Stir into cooking liquid. Cook and stir until sauce boils and thickens. Pour sauce over chicken.

Chicken Bordeaux

Servings: 4
Per Serving
Calories: 530
Fat: 29.4 g
Sodium: 358 mg
Cholesterol: 140 mg

3 pound chicken, cut into quarters
1 teaspoon coarse black pepper
3 tablespoons vegetable oil
1 whole clove garlic
1 cup dry white wine
1 (16-ounce) can tomatoes, undrained
1 (3-ounce) can sliced mushrooms, drained

Rub chicken with pepper. Heat oil and garlic in 6- or 8-quart pressure cooker over medium heat. Brown chicken and remove. Discard garlic. Stir in wine, tomatoes, and mushrooms. Return chicken to pressure cooker. Close cover securely. Place pressure regulator on vent pipe. COOK 8 MINUTES at 15 pounds pressure. Quick cool cooker. Remove chicken and boil cooking liquid to thicken, if desired.

● ● ● ● ● ● ●

California Chicken & Artichokes

Servings: 4
Per Serving
Calories: 345
Fat: 17 g
Sodium: 157 mg
Cholesterol: 135 mg

3 small to medium artichokes or 1 package frozen (thawed) artichokes
Lemon juice
3 tablespoons vegetable oil
2 chicken breasts, skinned, boned, cut into halves
Salt
Pepper
3 cloves garlic, peeled, sliced
1 teaspoon dried rosemary or 1 large sprig fresh rosemary
1 lemon, thinly sliced
¼ cup chopped parsley
¾ cup dry white wine
¾ cup water

✱ ✱ ✱ ✱ ✱

1 egg yolk
2 tablespoons whipping cream or milk

Remove tough outer leaves from artichokes. Cut off tops, leaving about 1 inch. Cut off stems and dark green part from bottoms. Cut into quarters. Remove inner purple leaves and fuzzy chokes. Rub cut surfaces with lemon juice. Heat oil in pressure cooker over medium heat. Brown chicken. Sprinkle with salt and pepper. Place garlic, rosemary, and lemon on top of chicken. Sprinkle with parsley. Arrange artichokes on top of chicken. Add wine and water. Close cover securely. Place pressure regulator on vent pipe. COOK 6 MINUTES at 15 pounds pressure. Let pressure drop of its own accord. Remove artichokes and chicken. Keep warm. Beat egg yolk with cream. Whisk in some of the hot pan juices. Whisk cream mixture into remaining pan juices. Cook over low heat, stirring constantly, until slightly thickened. Pour sauce over chicken.

Intro

Basics

Appetizers

Soups and Stocks

Meats

Poultry

Seafood

Vegetables

Breads

Desserts

Whole Meal Magic

Curried Chicken & Yogurt

1 (3- to 3½-pound) chicken, cut up
1½ cups water
½ cup plain yogurt
1 tablespoon lemon juice
2 cloves garlic, minced
2 teaspoons grated fresh ginger
  or ½ teaspoon ground ginger
1 teaspoon turmeric

1 teaspoon salt
1 teaspoon paprika
1 teaspoon curry powder
¼ teaspoon pepper
2 tablespoons cooking oil
* * * * *
2 tablespoons cornstarch
2 tablespoons cold water

Servings: 6
Per Serving
Calories: 310
Fat: 17.4 g
Sodium: 422 mg
Cholesterol: 95 mg

Place chicken in a single layer in a glass dish. Combine water, yogurt, lemon juice, garlic, ginger, turmeric, salt, paprika, curry powder, and pepper; pour over chicken and marinate at room temperature for one hour. Heat oil in pressure cooker over medium heat. Remove chicken from marinade, brushing off as much as possible. Brown chicken, a few pieces at a time. Return all chicken to cooker; pour marinade over chicken. Close cover securely. Place pressure regulator on vent pipe. COOK 8 MINUTES at 15 pounds pressure. Let pressure drop of its own accord. Remove chicken pieces to a warm platter. Mix cornstarch with cold water; stir into hot sauce. Cook and stir until mixture boils. Pour sauce over chicken.

● ● ● ● ● ● ●

Servings: 6
Per Serving
Calories: 351
Fat: 22.1 g
Sodium: 237 mg
Cholesterol: 144 mg

Chicken Fricassee with Herbs

2 tablespoons vegetable oil
1 (3- to 3½-pound) chicken, cut up
1½ cups water or chicken stock or broth
1 medium onion, cut into quarters
½ teaspoon salt
¼ teaspoon pepper

Pinch ground cloves
½ teaspoon fresh or ¼ teaspoon dried rosemary
½ teaspoon fresh or ¼ teaspoon dried marjoram
* * * * *
⅓ cup whipping cream
1 egg yolk
1 tablespoon all-purpose flour

Heat oil in pressure cooker over medium heat. Brown chicken, a few pieces at a time. Return all chicken to pressure cooker. Add water, onion, salt, pepper, cloves, rosemary, and marjoram. Close cover securely. Place pressure regulator on vent pipe. COOK 8 MINUTES at 15 pounds pressure. Let pressure drop of its own accord. Beat cream, egg yolk, and flour together until smooth. Push chicken to one side in pressure cooker. Whisk cream mixture into cooking liquid. Cook and stir until slightly thickened. Coat chicken pieces with sauce.

Chicken Cacciatore

3 tablespoons all-purpose flour
1 teaspoon salt
⅛ teaspoon pepper
1 (3- to 3½-pound) chicken, cut up
¼ cup diced salt pork
1½ cups sliced onions
2 tablespoons olive oil
½ teaspoon chopped fresh oregano or 1 teaspoon dried oregano
2 tablespoons minced parsley

2 cloves garlic, minced
1 (16-ounce) can whole plum tomatoes, undrained, chopped
½ cup chopped carrot
½ cup chopped celery
½ cup dry white wine
½ cup water
Salt
Pepper

* * * * *

1 (6-ounce) can tomato paste

Servings: 6
Per Serving
Calories: 386
Fat: 18.2 g
Sodium: 858 mg
Cholesterol: 97 mg

Mix flour, 1 teaspoon salt, and ⅛ teaspoon pepper. Coat chicken with flour mixture and set aside. Fry salt pork in pressure cooker over medium heat until crisp; remove. Add onions. Sauté until light brown and remove. Add oil and brown chicken, a few pieces at a time, and remove. Discard excess fat. Stir oregano, parsley, and garlic into remaining fat. Return chicken, salt pork, and onions to pressure cooker. Add tomatoes, carrot, celery, wine, and water. Sprinkle with salt and pepper. Close cover securely. Place pressure regulator on vent pipe. COOK 8 MINUTES at 15 pounds pressure. Let pressure drop of its own accord. Remove chicken. Keep warm. Stir in tomato paste and simmer until thickened. Serve sauce over chicken.

● ● ● ● ● ● ●

Chili Sauce Turkey Loaf

1 pound ground turkey
½ cup chopped onion
½ cup dry unseasoned bread crumbs
1 egg
3 tablespoons chili sauce
1 tablespoon horseradish mustard

2 teaspoons white Worcestershire sauce
1 large clove garlic, minced
½ teaspoon dried basil
½ teaspoon dried oregano
½ teaspoon salt
⅛ teaspoon pepper
2½ cups water

❋ *Low Calorie*
Servings: 4
Per Serving
Calories: 230
Fat: 10.5 g
Sodium: 610 mg
Cholesterol: 95 mg

Thoroughly mix all ingredients except water. Pack into 1-quart soufflé dish or ovenproof glass bowl that fits loosely on rack (or in basket) in pressure cooker. Cover dish securely with aluminum foil. Place cooking rack (or basket) and water in pressure cooker. Place soufflé dish on rack (or in basket). Close cover securely. Place pressure regulator on vent pipe. COOK 20 MINUTES at 15 pounds pressure. Quick cool cooker. Remove soufflé dish and drain liquid from dish. Unmold turkey loaf. Brush with chili sauce, if desired.

Intro

Basics

Appetizers

Soups and Stocks

Meats

Poultry

Seafood

Vegetables

Breads

Desserts

Whole Meal Magic

6.

Chicken a la Provence

1 cup diced white turnip	3½ pound whole chicken
½ cup diced smoked sausage or ham	1 (13¾-ounce) can single-strength chicken broth
1 clove garlic	1 cup water
1 egg	* * * * *
3 tablespoons grated Parmesan cheese	4 carrots, each cut into 4 pieces
4-5 sprigs parsley	2 celery stalks, each cut into 4 pieces
¼ teaspoon dried thyme	2 onions, each cut into quarters
¼ teaspoon ground nutmeg	

Servings: 6
Per Serving
Calories: 347
Fat: 15.6 g
Sodium: 451 mg
Cholesterol: 137 mg

Chop turnip, sausage, and garlic in food processor. Combine turnip mixture with egg, cheese, parsley, thyme, and nutmeg. Mix well. Pack loosely into chicken cavity. Pin and tie wings close to sides of chicken; tie legs together. Place cooking rack (or basket), chicken broth, and water in 6- or 8-quart pressure cooker. Place chicken on rack (or in basket). Close cover securely. Place pressure regulator on vent pipe. COOK 15 MINUTES at 15 pounds pressure. Quick cool cooker. Arrange carrots, celery, and onions around chicken. Close cover securely. Place pressure regulator on vent pipe. COOK 2 MINUTES at 15 pounds pressure. Let pressure drop of its own accord.

● ● ● ● ● ● ●

Chicken with Cracked Pepper

✿ *Low Calorie*
♥ *Low Cholesterol*
Servings: 4
Per Serving
Calories: 225
Fat: 7.1 g
Sodium: 316 mg
Cholesterol: 73 mg

(Shown on page 55)

2 chicken breasts, skinned, boned, cut into halves	¼ cup chopped chives or green onion tops
1-2 teaspoons cracked mixed peppercorns	* * * * *
1-2 tablespoons olive or vegetable oil	¼ cup packaged seasoned bread crumbs
1 cup chicken stock or broth	1 tablespoon lemon juice
½ cup water	1 tablespoon chopped parsley
2 tablespoons brandy, optional	1 teaspoon Worcestershire sauce
1 small clove garlic, minced	

Sprinkle chicken with pepper, pressing it into the flesh. Heat oil in pressure cooker over medium heat. Brown chicken and remove. Stir chicken stock, water, brandy, garlic, and chives into pressure cooker. Place cooking rack (or basket) in pressure cooker. Place chicken on rack (or in basket). Close cover securely. Place pressure regulator on vent pipe. COOK 3 MINUTES at 15 pounds pressure. Quick cool cooker. Remove chicken and rack (or basket). Keep warm. Stir bread crumbs, lemon juice, parsley, and Worcestershire sauce into cooking liquid and heat. Serve with chicken.

Oriental Chicken and Onions

❀ *Low Calorie*
Servings: 8
Per Serving
Calories: 233
Fat: 11.3 g
Sodium: 440 mg
Cholesterol: 70 mg

1 (3- to 3½-pound) chicken, cut up
⅔ cup teriyaki sauce
Water
1 medium sweet Spanish onion, cut into strips

1 large green pepper, cut into strips

* * * * *

1 tablespoon vegetable oil
3 tablespoons cornstarch
¼ cup water

Place chicken and teriyaki sauce in plastic bag. Close bag securely. Marinate in refrigerator 8 hours or overnight, turning bag over occasionally. Remove chicken from marinade. Pour marinade into measuring cup. Add enough water to marinade to measure 1½ cups. Place cooking rack (or basket) and marinade in 6- or 8-quart pressure cooker. Place chicken, skin side up, on rack (or in basket). Sprinkle with onion and half the green pepper. Close cover securely. Place pressure regulator on vent pipe. COOK 8 MINUTES at 15 pounds pressure. Let pressure drop of its own accord. Meanwhile, heat oil in frying pan over medium heat. Sauté remaining green pepper until crisp-tender and reserve. Remove chicken and vegetables; keep warm. Remove rack (or basket). Add enough water to cooking liquid to measure 2 cups. Mix cornstarch with ¼ cup water. Mix with cooking liquid. Cook and stir until sauce boils and thickens. Spoon sautéed pepper on top of chicken. Top with sauce.

● ● ● ● ● ● ●

Country Captain Chicken

Servings: 4
Per Serving
Calories: 489
Fat: 26 g
Sodium: 266 mg
Cholesterol: 140 mg

(Shown on page 60)

2 tablespoons vegetable oil
1 (3- to 3½-pound) chicken, cut up
1 small onion, diced
½ red or green pepper, diced
1½ teaspoons curry powder
½ teaspoon dried thyme
1 clove garlic, minced
1 (16-ounce) can whole tomatoes, undrained, chopped

1 cup water
3 tablespoons currants or chopped raisins

* * * * *

Salt
Pepper
Toasted blanched almonds, optional
Hot cooked rice

Heat oil in pressure cooker over medium heat. Brown chicken, a few pieces at a time, and remove. Stir onion, green pepper, curry powder, thyme, and garlic into pan drippings. Stir in tomatoes, water, and currants. Return chicken to pressure cooker. Close cover securely. Place pressure regulator on vent pipe. COOK 8 MINUTES at 15 pounds pressure. Quick cool cooker. Season to taste with salt and pepper. Sprinkle chicken with almonds. Serve with rice.

Intro

Basics

Appetizers

Soups
and
Stocks

Meats

Poultry

Seafood

Vegetables

Breads

Desserts

Whole
Meal
Magic

Turkey and Dumplings

2 pounds turkey wings
Salt
Pepper
2 cups water

⅓ cup cold water
1 cup chicken stock or broth
1 cup baking and pancake mix
  with buttermilk
⅓ cup milk

* * * * *

3 tablespoons all-purpose flour

Servings: 4
Per Serving
Calories: 358
Fat: 14.2 g
Sodium: 624 mg
Cholesterol: 111 mg

Sprinkle turkey wings lightly with salt and pepper. Place cooking rack (or basket) and 2 cups water in 6- or 8-quart pressure cooker. Place turkey wings on rack (or in basket). Close cover securely. Place pressure regulator on vent pipe. COOK 20 MINUTES at 15 pounds pressure. Let pressure drop of its own accord. Remove turkey wings and rack (or basket). Reserve 1 cup cooking liquid. Cool turkey. Remove turkey meat from bones. Discard skin and bones. Cut turkey into bite-size pieces. Mix flour with ⅓ cup cold water. Mix with chicken stock and reserved cooking liquid in pressure cooker. Cook and stir until mixture boils and thickens. Stir in turkey. Season to taste with salt and pepper. Mix baking mix and milk. Drop batter by spoonfuls onto simmering turkey mixture. Close cover securely. Do not place pressure regulator on vent pipe. COOK 12-15 MINUTES with steam flowing very gently through vent pipe.

●　●　●　●　●　●　●

Servings: 6
Per Serving
Calories: 303
Fat: 17.4 g
Sodium: 422 mg
Cholesterol: 95 mg

East Indian Chicken

1 (3- to 3½-pound) chicken,
  cut up
1½ cups water
½ cup plain yogurt
1 tablespoon lemon juice
2 cloves garlic, minced
2 teaspoons grated fresh ginger
1 teaspoon ground turmeric

1 teaspoon salt
1 teaspoon paprika
1 teaspoon curry powder
¼ teaspoon pepper
2 tablespoons vegetable oil

* * * * *

2 teaspoons cornstarch
2 teaspoons cold water

Place chicken in single layer in shallow glass casserole. Mix 1½ cups water, yogurt, lemon juice, garlic, ginger, turmeric, salt, paprika, curry powder, and pepper. Pour over chicken. Marinate in refrigerator 1 hour. Remove chicken from marinade, brushing off and reserving as much marinade as possible. Heat oil in pressure cooker over medium heat. Brown chicken, a few pieces at a time. Return all chicken to pressure cooker. Pour reserved marinade over chicken. Close cover securely. Place pressure regulator on vent pipe. COOK 8 MINUTES at 15 pounds pressure. Let pressure drop of its own accord. Remove chicken. Keep warm. Mix cornstarch with 2 teaspoons cold water. Stir into cooking liquid. Cook and stir until sauce boils and thickens. Pour sauce over chicken.

Sweet 'n Sour Chicken

1 tablespoon vegetable oil
1 (3- to 3½-pound) chicken, cut up
1 green or red pepper, cut into chunks
½ cup sliced celery
1 (20-ounce) can pineapple chunks, drained, juice reserved
   Water
½ cup cider vinegar
¼ cup packed brown sugar
2 tablespoons soy sauce
1 tablespoon catsup
½ teaspoon Worcestershire sauce
¼ teaspoon ground ginger

* * * * *

2 tablespoons cornstarch
2 tablespoons cold water

Servings: 6
Per Serving
Calories: 353
Fat: 15 g
Sodium: 443 mg
Cholesterol: 93 mg

(Shown on page 49)

Heat oil in pressure cooker over medium heat. Brown chicken, a few pieces at a time, and remove. Return all chicken to pressure cooker. Add green pepper and celery. Add enough water to reserved pineapple juice to measure 1 cup. Mix with vinegar, brown sugar, soy sauce, catsup, Worcestershire sauce, and ginger. Pour over chicken. Close cover securely. Place pressure regulator on vent pipe. COOK 8 MINUTES at 15 pounds pressure. Let pressure drop of its own accord. Remove chicken and vegetables. Keep warm. Mix cornstarch with 2 tablespoons cold water. Stir into cooking liquid. Cook and stir until sauce boils and thickens. Add pineapple chunks. Cook until hot. Pour sauce over chicken. Serve over rice, if desired.

● ● ● ● ● ● ●

Chicken Couscous with Raspberry Vinegar

2 chicken breasts, skinned, boned, cut into halves
   Salt
   Pepper
2-3 tablespoons olive or vegetable oil
½ pound shallots or small pearl onions
1 cup chicken stock or broth
3 tablespoons raspberry or red wine vinegar
⅓ cup water

* * * * *

¾ cup quick-cooking couscous or instant rice
½ cup fresh or frozen (thawed) raspberries

♥ **Low Cholesterol**
Servings: 4
Per Serving
Calories: 390
Fat: 10.5 g
Sodium: 267 mg
Cholesterol: 73 mg

(Shown on page 156)

Sprinkle chicken with salt and pepper. Heat oil in pressure cooker over medium heat. Brown chicken. Add shallots, chicken stock, vinegar, and water. Close cover securely. Place pressure regulator on vent pipe. COOK 3 MINUTES at 15 pounds pressure. Quick cool cooker. Remove chicken. Keep warm. Heat stock mixture to boiling. Stir in couscous. Remove from heat. Let stand 5 minutes. Gently stir in raspberries. Serve with chicken.

Intro

Basics

Appetizers

Soups and Stocks

Meats

Poultry

Seafood

Vegetables

Breads

Desserts

Whole Meal Magic

6. *Coq Au Vin*

4 slices bacon, diced	2 teaspoons minced parsley
½ pound mushrooms, sliced	1 clove garlic, minced
1 (3- to 3½-pound) chicken, cut up	1 small bay leaf
1 medium onion, sliced	* * * * *
1 medium carrot, sliced	1 (16-ounce) can pearl onions, drained
1 cup dry red wine	¼ cup brandy
½ cup water	Salt
1 teaspoon chopped fresh basil or ½ teaspoon dried basil	Pepper

Servings: 6
Per Serving
Calories: 356
Fat: 15 g
Sodium: 200 mg
Cholesterol: 97 mg

Fry bacon in pressure cooker over medium heat until crisp. Remove and reserve. Add mushrooms and sauté. Remove and reserve. Brown chicken, a few pieces at a time, and remove. Sauté sliced onion and carrot. Return all chicken to pressure cooker. Combine wine, water, basil, parsley, garlic, and bay leaf. Pour over chicken. Close cover securely. Place pressure regulator on vent pipe. COOK 8 MINUTES at 15 pounds pressure. Let pressure drop of its own accord. Remove chicken, onion, and carrot. Keep warm. Add reserved mushrooms and canned onions to pressure cooker. Cook until hot. Add brandy and reserved bacon. Season to taste with salt and pepper. Cook until hot. Pour sauce over chicken and vegetables.

● ● ● ● ● ●

Chicken Breasts with Tarragon

❀ *Low Calorie*
Servings: 2
Per Serving
Calories: 127
Fat: 4.5 g
Sodium: 41 mg
Cholesterol: 71.5 mg

1 chicken breast, cut into halves	¼ cup diced onion
Salt	1 teaspoon dried tarragon
Pepper	* * * * *
1 cup dry white wine	1 egg yolk
½ cup water	¼ cup whipping cream
¼ cup diced celery	1 teaspoon cornstarch
¼ cup diced carrot	2 slices toast, optional

Sprinkle chicken with salt and pepper. Place chicken, wine, water, celery, carrot, onion, and tarragon in pressure cooker. Close cover securely. Place pressure regulator on vent pipe. COOK 6 MINUTES at 15 pounds pressure. Quick cool cooker. Remove chicken. Keep warm. Strain cooking liquid and return to pressure cooker. Cook until reduced to ½ cup. Mix egg yolk, cream, and cornstarch. Whisk some of the hot broth into cream mixture. Whisk cream mixture into remaining broth in pressure cooker. Cook and whisk over medium heat until thickened. Place chicken on toast. Spoon sauce over chicken.

Herbed Chicken with Potatoes

Servings: 4
Per Serving
Calories: 614
Fat: 26.2 g
Sodium: 285 mg
Cholesterol: 140 mg

(Shown on page 145)

2 (2-inch) sprigs rosemary or ½
   teaspoon dried rosemary
1 (3- to 3½-pound) chicken
   Salt
   Pepper
   Paprika
2 tablespoons olive oil
1 head garlic (20 or 30 cloves)

4 medium new potatoes
½ cup chicken broth
½ cup white wine (may
   substitute broth)
1 cup water

* * * * *

2 tablespoons flour
¼ cup chicken broth or water

Place a rosemary sprig or ¼ teaspoon dried rosemary in cavity of chicken. Truss chicken, tying legs and wings securely to the body. Season with salt, pepper, and paprika. Heat oil in 6- or 8-quart pressure cooker over medium heat; brown chicken on all sides, using the string to assist in turning. Remove chicken. Separate garlic into cloves; remove skin. Cut potatoes in half, if desired. Brown garlic and potatoes in hot oil; remove potatoes. Place cooking rack (or basket) in cooker. Put chicken on cooking rack (or in basket), breast side up. Arrange potatoes around sides of chicken. Add broth, wine, and water. Do not fill cooker over ⅔ full. Sprinkle chicken with remaining rosemary. Close cover securely. Place pressure regulator on vent pipe. COOK 15 MINUTES at 15 pounds pressure. Let pressure drop of its own accord. Remove chicken and potatoes; keep warm. Remove rack (or basket). Discard garlic. Mix flour with ¼ cup chicken broth and add to hot juices in cooker. Cook and stir until thickened, adding more broth if desired. Serve with chicken and potatoes.

NOTE: *Cut up chicken may be used.*

Intro

Basics

Appetizers

Soups
and
Stocks

Meats

Poultry

Seafood

Vegetables

Breads

Desserts

Whole
Meal
Magic

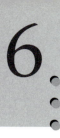

6. *Chicken Pot Pie*

1 (3- to 3½-pound) chicken, cut up
2 cups water
¾ teaspoon salt
⅛ teaspoon pepper
⅛ teaspoon saffron or ground turmeric

* * * * *

6 small white onions
½ cup sliced celery
½ cup julienne-cut carrot
½ teaspoon fresh thyme or ¼ teaspoon dried thyme

* * * * *

¼ cup all-purpose flour
2 tablespoons butter, melted
¼ cup sour cream
Pastry for single crust
Cream or beaten egg yolk
Fresh sage leaves, optional

Servings: 6
Per Serving
Calories: 425
Fat: 25.3 g
Sodium: 424 mg
Cholesterol: 143 mg

(Shown on page 159)

Combine chicken, water, salt, pepper, and saffron in 6- or 8-quart pressure cooker. Close cover securely. Place pressure regulator on vent pipe. COOK 8 MINUTES at 15 pounds pressure. Let pressure drop of its own accord. Remove chicken and cool slightly. Strain cooking liquid. Skim off fat. Measure 2 cups and pour into pressure cooker. Add onions, celery, carrot, and thyme. Close cover securely. Place pressure regulator on vent pipe. COOK 3 MINUTES at 15 pounds pressure. Quick cool cooker. Remove skin and bones from chicken. Cut chicken into large pieces. Add chicken to pressure cooker. Heat to simmering. Mix flour with butter. Whisk into chicken mixture. Cook and stir until mixture boils and thickens. Remove from heat. Stir in sour cream. Pour hot mixture into 2-quart casserole. Roll out pastry to cover top of casserole. Crimp edges, if desired. Brush pastry with cream. Arrange sage leaves on pastry. Bake in 450 degree F oven for 15 to 20 minutes, until browned.

Turkey Sausage with Potato Salad

❀ *Low Calorie*
Servings: 6
Per Serving
Calories: 289
Fat: 15.3 g
Sodium: 395 mg
Cholesterol: 28 mg

(Shown on page 145)

1 **pound ground turkey**
⅓ **cup quick cooking oats**
2 **tablespoons minced parsley**
1 **tablespoon lemon juice**
2 **small cloves garlic, minced**
½ **teaspoon salt**
½ **teaspoon pepper**
¼ **teaspoon ground allspice**
¼ **teaspoon red pepper sauce**
3 **cups water**

* * * * *
8 **small red-skinned potatoes**
* * * * *
¼ **cup olive oil**
1 **small onion or 2 shallots, minced**
3 **tablespoons red wine vinegar**
½ **teaspoon salt**
¼ **teaspoon dry mustard**

Mix turkey, oats, 1 tablespoon of the parsley, lemon juice, garlic, ½ teaspoon salt, pepper, allspice, and red pepper sauce. Shape into a 7-inch roll. Place on 12-inch long piece of aluminum foil. Bring long sides of foil up and fold them together to seal closely on top of roll. Twist the two ends to seal. With sharp long-tined fork or thin knife, make holes on all sides of roll, turning to keep round shape. Place cooking rack (or basket) and water in 6- or 8-quart pressure cooker. Place roll, seam side up, on rack (or in basket). Close cover securely. Place pressure regulator on vent pipe. COOK 12 MINUTES at 15 pounds pressure. Quick cool cooker. Place potatoes on rack (or in basket) along sides of sausage roll. Close cover securely. Place pressure regulator on vent pipe. COOK 8 MINUTES at 15 pounds pressure. Let pressure drop of its own accord. Remove potatoes, sausage, and water. Cool potatoes under cold water. Peel potatoes and chop coarsely. Heat oil in pressure cooker over medium heat; sauté onion until tender. Whisk vinegar, ½ teaspoon salt, mustard, and remaining 1 tablespoon parsley into onion mixture. Pour over potatoes. Mix gently. Remove foil from sausage roll and slice. Serve warm sausage with potato salad.

NOTE: *Potato salad may be omitted. Pressure cook sausage roll for a total of 20 minutes.*

Intro

Basics

Appetizers

Soups
and
Stocks

Meats

Poultry

Seafood

Vegetables

Breads

Desserts

Whole
Meal
Magic

6. *Jambalaya*

1 tablespoon olive or vegetable oil
2 chicken breast halves, boned, skinned, cut into halves
8 ounces cooked smoked sausage, cut into 1-inch pieces
1 cup chopped onion
1 cup thinly sliced celery
½ cup chopped red or green pepper
1 cup fresh or frozen (thawed) whole okra
1 bay leaf
½ teaspoon dried thyme
1 teaspoon salt

¼ teaspoon black pepper
⅛-¼ teaspoon cayenne pepper
1 (16-ounce) can whole tomatoes, undrained
Chicken stock

* * * * *

3 cups cooked long grain rice, warm
8 ounces shrimp, peeled, deveined
1 cup frozen peas, thawed
Salt
Pepper
Red pepper sauce

Servings: 6
Per Serving
Calories: 482
Fat: 17.3 g
Sodium: 1250 mg
Cholesterol: 138 mg

Heat oil in 6- or 8-quart pressure cooker over medium heat. Sauté chicken and sausage until chicken is lightly browned. Remove meat from pressure cooker; drain excess fat. Add onion, celery, red pepper, okra, bay leaf, thyme, salt, and pepper; sauté until onion is tender. Drain tomato liquid into 1-quart measure; coarsely chop tomatoes. Add enough chicken stock to tomato liquid to measure 2 cups; add tomatoes, liquid, and meat to pressure cooker. Close cover securely. Place pressure regulator on vent pipe. COOK 3 MINUTES at 15 pounds pressure. Let pressure drop of its own accord. Stir in rice, shrimp, and peas; cook uncovered over medium heat until shrimp are cooked, 3 to 4 minutes. Season to taste with salt, pepper, and red pepper sauce.

Arroz Con Pollo

1 (3- to 3½-pound) chicken, cut up
Paprika
Salt
Pepper
2 tablespoons olive oil
2 medium onions, chopped
1 clove garlic, minced
1 (13½-ounce) can single-strength chicken broth
½ cup water
1 bay leaf
½ teaspoon crushed red pepper

¼ teaspoon crushed saffron threads

* * * * *

1 (10-ounce) package frozen green peas
1 cup sliced green olives
1 tomato, peeled, chopped
1 (4-ounce) jar pimientos, drained, sliced

* * * * *

2 cups cooked long grain rice, warm

Servings: 6
Per Serving
Calories: 462
Fat: 19.3 g
Sodium: 521 mg
Cholesterol: 93 mg

(Shown on page 59)

Sprinkle chicken with paprika, salt, and pepper. Heat oil in 6- or 8-quart pressure cooker over medium heat. Brown chicken, a few pieces at a time, and remove. Add onions and garlic to pressure cooker. Sauté until tender. Return chicken to pressure cooker. Add chicken broth, water, bay leaf, red pepper, and saffron. Close cover securely. Place pressure regulator on vent pipe. COOK 8 MINUTES at 15 pounds pressure. Quick cool cooker. Remove chicken. Stir in peas, olives, tomato, and pimientos. Return chicken to pressure cooker. Close cover securely. Place pressure regulator on vent pipe. COOK 0 MINUTES. Let pressure drop of its own accord. Stir in cooked rice.

Intro

Basics

Appetizers

Soups and Stocks

Meats

Poultry

Seafood

Vegetables

Breads

Desserts

Whole Meal Magic

6. *Indonesian Chicken Stew*

1 tablespoon vegetable oil
1½ cups sliced mushrooms
1 cup chopped green pepper
¼ cup sliced green onion
1 small jalapeño chile, seeded, deveined, finely chopped
1 large clove garlic, minced
1 teaspoon minced fresh ginger
1 tablespoon sesame or vegetable oil
1 pound boneless skinless chicken, cut into ¾-inch pieces

½ cup sliced water chestnuts
2 tablespoons light soy sauce
1-2 tablespoons lime juice
1½ cups chicken stock or broth

1 cup canned unsweetened coconut milk*
Cayenne pepper
Cilantro, minced
Hot cooked rice

❀ *Low Calorie*
Servings: 6
Per Serving
Calories: 256
Fat: 16 g
Sodium: 413 mg
Cholesterol: 30 mg

Heat oil in pressure cooker over medium heat. Sauté mushrooms, green pepper, green onion, chile, garlic, and ginger until green pepper is tender. Remove vegetable mixture and reserve. Heat sesame oil in pressure cooker. Sauté chicken until no longer pink in the center, 2 to 3 minutes. Stir in water chestnuts, soy sauce, and lime juice. Stir in reserved vegetable mixture and chicken stock. Close cover securely. Place pressure regulator on vent pipe. COOK 5 MINUTES at 15 pounds pressure. Quick cool cooker. Stir in coconut milk. Cook over medium heat until hot. Season to taste with cayenne. Sprinkle with cilantro. Serve with rice.

*Coconut milk can be purchased in Oriental grocery stores and in the specialty departments of many supermarkets.

Lemon-Herbed Chicken

1 (3- to 3½-pound) chicken,
   cut up
   Salt
   Pepper
2-4 tablespoons olive oil
1 medium onion, chopped
1 tablespoon chopped garlic
1 cup chicken stock or broth
¼ cup water
1 cup chopped parsley
½ cup chopped celery leaves

¼ cup lemon juice
2 teaspoons chopped fresh
   oregano or 1 teaspoon dried
   oregano
1 teaspoon chopped fresh basil
   or ½ teaspoon dried basil

* * * * *

2 tablespoons all-purpose flour
2 tablespoons cold water
1 cup pitted ripe olives

Servings: 6
Per Serving
Calories: 331
Fat: 19.2 g
Sodium: 239 mg
Cholesterol: 93 mg

Sprinkle chicken with salt and pepper. Heat oil in pressure cooker over medium heat. Sauté onion and garlic until tender and remove. Brown chicken, a few pieces at a time, and remove. Return all chicken and onion mixture to pressure cooker. Add remaining ingredients except flour, 2 tablespoons water, and olives. Close cover securely. Place pressure regulator on vent pipe. COOK 8 MINUTES at 15 pounds pressure. Let pressure drop of its own accord. Remove chicken. Keep warm. Mix flour with 2 tablespoons cold water. Stir into cooking liquid in pressure cooker. Add olives. Cook and stir until mixture boils and thickens. Pour sauce over chicken.

Intro

Basics

Appetizers

Soups
and
Stocks

Meats

Poultry

Seafood

Vegetables

Breads

Desserts

Whole
Meal
Magic

Chinese Chicken Salad

2 chicken breasts, boned,
  skinned and cut in half
2 teaspoons soy sauce
1½ cups water
1 teaspoon dry ginger
½ teaspoon onion salt
2 tablespoons lemon juice
1 teaspoon rice or wine vinegar
¼ teaspoon sugar
⅛ teaspoon dry mustard

* * * * *

Select as desired:
Salad greens,
Pea pods, cooked and cooled
Fresh bean sprouts, washed
  and cleaned
Radish slices
2 teaspoons toasted sesame
  seeds

❀ *Low Calorie*
♥ *Low Cholesterol*

Servings: 6
Per Serving
Calories: 156
Fat: 3.7 g
Sodium: 390 mg
Cholesterol: 76 mg

(Shown on page 52)

Brush chicken with soy sauce. Combine water, ginger, onion salt, lemon juice, vinegar, sugar, and mustard. Place chicken and water mixture in pressure cooker. Close cover securely. Place pressure regulator on vent pipe. COOK 5 MINUTES at 15 pounds pressure. Quick cool cooker. Remove chicken. Set aside. Cooking liquid may be reserved and served warm over salad or thickened with cornstarch and served as sauce over salad, if desired.

To assemble salad: Arrange greens, pea pods, bean sprouts, and radish slices as desired on a serving platter. Slice chicken and decoratively arrange over greens. Serve with reserved sauce and sprinkle with sesame seeds.

7. Seafood

Like the tides, fish and seafood have come in and out of culinary fashion in America several times over the years. The earliest English settlers, who found themselves on the Atlantic coast after never having lived by the sea before, were understandably skeptical of the strange fish, lobsters, crabs, clams, oysters, and scallops they found in their new homeland. Their attitude soon turned to casual indifference, however, as they became spoiled by America's abundance from the sea.

The bounty of seafood available along the Atlantic formed the basis for much of the colonial cuisine—from fish chowders to boiled lobsters, cod cakes, creamed oysters, and salmon mousse. Dishes we now think of as "gourmet delicacies" were commonplace in even the most modest homes.

But as American expansion turned westward and inland, foods like meat and poultry that could be raised on land became more important to survival. The result was a culinary divide. If you lived by a waterway—an ocean, lake, or river—seafood was a popular and prevalent part of your food heritage. Marylanders ate crab cakes. In New Orleans, the citizens feasted on oyster etouffe, and New England residents considered cod a staple of their diets. If you were land-locked, however, these same foods were oddities.

7

This culinary division lasted well into the twentieth century, when technology finally made the transport and storage of seafood possible, practical, and safe. Unfortunately, by the time fish and shellfish were available everywhere, there were many homemakers who, lacking experience, feared fish cookery. For many, their first attempts at using the blocks of frozen fish fillets, found at their supermarkets, only served to confirm their fears.

The growing interest in travel, foreign cuisine, and gourmet cooking finally helped seafood gain favor in the sixties and seventies. The greatest boon to fish consumption in this country has come only in the last decade or so and its source was not chefs or trendsetters, but doctors, nutritionists, and dietitians.

Once we were convinced of the many health benefits of eating more fish, seafood became firmly ensconced in our food repertoire. Now, seafood restaurants are growing in number, and supermarket seafood departments are offering an incredible variety of fresh fish from around the world. Today, more and more homemakers make fish a regular part of the weekly menu plan.

Since fish cookery is unusually fast, most folks don't think of using the pressure cooker, but the fabulous flavors that result will soon convince you that many fish dishes shouldn't be prepared any other way. The only secret to success is scrupulous timing, since the difference between fish that is done to perfection and fish that is hopelessly overdone can be a matter of seconds.

If you lack the confidence to cook fish at home, the following recipes will prove how quick, easy, and delicious pressure cooked seafood can be. And there's one for every taste—from the light to the rich, from the hearty to the heart-smart. Some of our favorites are *Creole Cod, Crab-Stuffed Fish Fillets,* and *Orange Roughy & Oysters in Parchment.*

Crab-Stuffed Fish Fillets

¾ cup canned or frozen (thawed) crabmeat, flaked
¼ cup chopped pecans
2 tablespoons chopped green onion
2 tablespoons finely chopped celery
1 pound sole or other thin fish fillets, cut into 4 pieces
   Salt
   White pepper
½ cup dry white wine
1 cup water

* * * * *

1 tablespoon all-purpose flour
2 tablespoons cold water
⅓ cup whipping cream
¼ cup shredded Swiss cheese
   Lemon wedges

❀ Low Calorie
Servings: 4
Per Serving
Calories: 229
Fat: 11.9 g
Sodium: 173 mg
Cholesterol: 94 mg

Combine crabmeat, pecans, green onion, and celery. Sprinkle both sides of fish lightly with salt and pepper. Spread each piece of fish with about ¼ cup crab mixture. Roll up fish and secure with toothpick. Place greased cooking rack (or basket), wine, and 1 cup water in pressure cooker. Place fish rolls on rack (or in basket). Close cover securely. Place pressure regulator on vent pipe. COOK 7 MINUTES at 15 pounds pressure. Quick cool cooker. Remove fish and rack (or basket). Keep warm. Mix flour with 2 tablespoons cold water. Stir into sauce in pressure cooker. Heat to boiling. Stir in cream. Cook and stir until sauce boils and thickens. Remove pressure cooker from heat. Stir in cheese until melted. Spoon sauce over fish. Garnish with lemon wedges.

● ● ● ● ● ● ●

Fish in Salsa Ranchero

3 tablespoons olive oil
1 onion, sliced
1 clove garlic, minced
2 tomatoes, peeled, chopped or 1 pound tomatillos, chopped
1½ cups water
½ green pepper, finely chopped
1 tablespoon minced parsley
1 tablespoon minced cilantro
½ teaspoon salt
¼ teaspoon cumin seeds
¼ teaspoon dried oregano
1 (1-pound) package frozen cod fillets, thawed

* * * * *

Corn or flour tortillas

❀ Low Calorie
Servings: 4
Per Serving
Calories: 206
Fat: 11.1 g
Sodium: 337 mg
Cholesterol: 45 mg

Heat oil in pressure cooker over medium heat. Sauté onion and garlic until tender. Add tomatoes and water. Heat to boiling. Add green pepper, parsley, cilantro, salt, cumin, and oregano. Cut fish block into 4 even pieces. Place fish in sauce. Close cover securely. Place pressure regulator on vent pipe. COOK 2 MINUTES at 15 pounds pressure. Quick cool cooker. Cut 2 or 3 tortillas into thin strips. Stir them into mixture. Serve in bowls with additional warm tortillas.

Intro

Basics

Appetizers

Soups and Stocks

Meats

Poultry

Seafood

Vegetables

Breads

Desserts

Whole Meal Magic

Linguini with Calamari Sauce

½ cup fish stock
1 cup water
2 tablespoons olive oil
2 cloves garlic, minced
½ teaspoon salt

1 tablespoon minced parsley
1 pound cleaned squid, cut
  into ¼-inch rings*

* * * * *

Cooked linguini

❋ Low Calorie
Servings: 4
Per Serving
Calories: 166
Fat: 8.3 g
Sodium: 341 mg
Cholesterol: 266 mg

Combine fish stock, water, oil, garlic, and salt in pressure cooker. Heat to boiling. Add parsley and squid. Close cover securely. Place pressure regulator on vent pipe. COOK 1 MINUTE at 15 pounds pressure. Quick cool cooker. Serve squid and sauce over linguini.

*Fresh or canned chopped clams can be substituted for the squid.

Catfish Creole

❋ Low Calorie
Servings: 4
Per Serving
Calories: 292
Fat: 12 g
Sodium: 317 mg
Cholesterol: 65 mg

2 tablespoons olive or
  vegetable oil
1 cup chopped onion
½ cup chopped green pepper
½ cup sliced celery
½ cup fresh or frozen (thawed)
  cut okra
2-3 cloves garlic, minced
½ teaspoon dried marjoram
½ teaspoon crushed celery seeds
¼ teaspoon dried thyme
¼ teaspoon ground cumin
1 bay leaf

1 tablespoon all-purpose flour
1 cup dry white wine or
  chicken stock or broth
½ cup water
4 catfish fillets (about 1 pound)

* * * * *

1 (16-ounce) can whole
  tomatoes, drained, chopped
2 tablespoons tomato paste

* * * * *

Salt
Pepper

Heat oil in pressure cooker over medium heat. Sauté onion, green pepper, celery, okra, garlic, and herbs until onions are tender. Stir in flour. Cook 1 minute. Remove vegetable mixture and reserve. Place greased cooking rack (or basket), wine, and water in pressure cooker. Place fish on rack (or in basket). Close cover securely. Place pressure regulator on vent pipe. COOK 2 MINUTES at 15 pounds pressure. Quick cool cooker. Remove fish and rack (or basket). Keep warm. Mix tomatoes, tomato paste, and reserved vegetable mixture with liquid in pressure cooker. Close cover securely. Place pressure regulator on vent pipe. COOK 0 MINUTES. Quick cool cooker. Season sauce to taste with salt and pepper. Serve sauce over fish.

Saffron Fish Stew

1 pound firm fish (halibut, haddock, cod, pollack, etc.), fresh or thawed
¼ cup dry white wine
1 medium onion, finely chopped (about 1 cup)
2 cloves garlic, minced
¼ cup chopped parsley
1 bay leaf
8 small new red potatoes
3 carrots, cut into ½-inch chunks
1 (14½-ounce) can chicken broth
Pinch of saffron threads or ¼ teaspoon turmeric

* * * * *

1 small red pepper, cut into chunks
1 cup frozen peas, thawed

❀ *Low Calorie*
♥ *Low Cholesterol*
Servings: 8
Per Serving
Calories: 174
Fat: 1 g
Sodium: 270 mg
Cholesterol: 40 mg

(Shown on page 63)

Cut fish into 8 chunks. Place wine, onion, garlic, parsley, and bay leaf in pressure cooker. Add fish and turn to coat. Let marinate while preparing vegetables. Scrub potatoes and remove one strip of peeling around each. Put potatoes and carrots in pressure cooker. Add chicken broth and saffron. Close cover securely. Place pressure regulator on vent pipe. COOK 2 MINUTES at 15 pounds pressure. Quick cool cooker. Stir in red pepper and peas. Close cover securely. Place pressure regulator on vent pipe. COOK 1 MINUTE at 15 pounds pressure. Quick cool cooker. Discard bay leaf.

● ● ● ● ● ● ●

Sauced Scallops

½ cup dry white wine
1 cup water
1 pound sea scallops

* * * * *

½ cup whipping cream
½ cup chopped tomato
1 teaspoon crushed anise seeds
¼ teaspoon sugar
Salt
1 teaspoon margarine

❀ *Low Calorie*
Servings: 4
Per Serving
Calories: 216
Fat: 10.6 g
Sodium: 207 mg
Cholesterol: 71 mg

Place cooking rack (or basket), wine, and water in pressure cooker. Place scallops on rack (or in basket). Close cover securely. Place pressure regulator on vent pipe. COOK 2 MINUTES at 15 pounds pressure. Quick cool cooker. Remove scallops and rack (or basket). Keep warm. Stir cream, tomato, anise seeds, and sugar into wine. Heat to boiling. Reduce heat and simmer rapidly, uncovered, until sauce is reduced to 1 cup. Season to taste with salt. Stir in margarine. Spoon sauce over scallops.

Intro
Basics
Appetizers
Soups and Stocks
Meats
Poultry
Seafood
Vegetables
Breads
Desserts
Whole Meal Magic

7

Orange Roughy & Oysters in Parchment

2 slices bacon, diced	Pepper
½ cup chopped red pepper	8 medium oysters, shucked
¼ cup chopped green onion	¼ cup butter, melted
1 pound orange roughy, cut into 4 pieces	½ cup soda cracker crumbs
Salt	1½ cups water

Servings: 4
Per Serving
Calories: 483
Fat: 35.5 g
Sodium: 620 mg
Cholesterol: 176 mg

Fry bacon in 6- or 8-quart pressure cooker over medium heat until crisp. Remove bacon and reserve. Discard all but 1 tablespoon fat. Add red pepper and green onion. Sauté until tender. Remove vegetables and reserve. Cut four 12-inch squares of parchment paper or aluminum foil. Sprinkle fish lightly on both sides with salt and pepper. Place each piece on square of parchment. Dip oysters in butter. Coat with cracker crumbs. Place 2 oysters on each piece of fish. Sprinkle oysters with reserved vegetable mixture. Fold tops and sides of parchment butcher-style to make sealed packets. Place cooking rack (or basket) and water in pressure cooker. Place packets on rack (or in basket). Close cover securely. Place pressure regulator on vent pipe. COOK 6 MINUTES at 15 pounds pressure. Quick cool cooker. Open packets. Garnish with reserved bacon.

• • • • • • •

❧ **Low Calorie**
Servings: 4
Per Serving
Calories: 152
Fat: 5.8 g
Sodium: 474 mg
Cholesterol: 178 mg

Shrimp and Snow Peas

1 tablespoon vegetable oil	½ teaspoon salt
4 ounces snow peas	¼ teaspoon pepper
¼ cup sliced red pepper	1½ cups water
1-2 cloves garlic, minced	* * * * *
1 pound medium shrimp, shelled, deveined	3-4 tablespoons half-and-half
1 cup chopped tomato	Cooked tortellini or other pasta

Heat oil in pressure cooker over medium heat. Sauté snow peas, red pepper, and garlic until tender. Stir in shrimp, tomato, salt, pepper, and water. Close cover securely. Place pressure regulator on vent pipe. COOK 2 MINUTES at 15 pounds pressure. Quick cool cooker. Drain off excess liquid. Stir in half-and-half. Serve over tortellini.

Salmon Steaks Moutarde

4 small salmon steaks, 1 inch thick*
4 tablespoons Dijon-style mustard
3-4 sprigs fresh thyme or ½ teaspoon dried thyme
1 tablespoon olive or vegetable oil
1 onion, chopped
1 clove garlic, minced
1 cup dry white wine or chicken stock or broth
½ cup water
1 bay leaf

2 tablespoons Dijon-style mustard
1 tablespoon cornstarch

✿ *Low Calorie*
Servings: 4
Per Serving
Calories: 218
Fat: 8.7 g
Sodium: 1004 mg
Cholesterol: 20 mg

(Shown on page 55)

Spread each steak with 1 tablespoon mustard. Press 1 thyme sprig into mustard on each steak or sprinkle with dried thyme. Heat oil in pressure cooker over medium heat. Sauté onion and garlic until tender. Stir in wine, water, and bay leaf. Place cooking rack (or basket) in pressure cooker. Place steaks on rack (or in basket). Close cover securely. Place pressure regulator on vent pipe. COOK 4 MINUTES at 15 pounds pressure. Quick cool cooker. Carefully remove steaks and rack (or basket). Keep warm. Discard bay leaf. Mix 2 tablespoons mustard with cornstarch. Stir into liquid in pressure cooker. Cook and stir until sauce boils and thickens. Serve sauce with salmon steaks.

*Other thick fish such as halibut may be used.

Intro

Basics

Appetizers

Soups and Stocks

Meats

Poultry

Seafood

Vegetables

Breads

Desserts

Whole Meal Magic

117

Creole Cod

¼ cup olive oil
2 cups chopped sweet Spanish onions
1 large green pepper, chopped
1 cup chopped celery
2 cloves garlic, minced
1 (28-ounce) can whole tomatoes, undrained
 Water

¼ cup dry white wine
2 bay leaves
2 (1-pound) cod fillets, fresh or frozen (thawed)

⅓ cup soy sauce
1 tablespoon paprika
¼ teaspoon cayenne pepper
 Hot cooked rice

✿ *Low Calorie*

Servings: 8
Per Serving
Calories: 197
Fat: 7.8 g
Sodium: 925 mg
Cholesterol: 45 mg

(Shown on page 151)

Heat oil in 6- or 8-quart pressure cooker over medium heat. Sauté onions, green pepper, celery, and garlic until tender. Remove vegetables and reserve. Drain liquid from tomatoes adding water to measure 1¼ cups. Pour into pressure cooker. Add wine and bay leaves. Place cooking rack (or basket) in pressure cooker. Place cod fillets on rack (or in basket) in crisscross fashion. (They will not lie flat. Do not, however, allow fish to extend above the ⅔ full level in pressure cooker). Close cover securely. Place pressure regulator on vent pipe. COOK 2 MINUTES at 15 pounds pressure. Quick cool cooker. Remove fish and rack (or basket). Chop tomatoes. Stir tomatoes, reserved vegetables, soy sauce, paprika, and cayenne pepper into cooking liquid. Add fish, breaking into large chunks. Heat to boiling. Simmer 1 minute. Discard bay leaves. Serve with rice.

Tuna Mediterranean

1 tablespoon olive or vegetable oil
2 tuna, bluefish, swordfish, or halibut steaks, cut into halves (about 1 pound)
Garlic salt
Pepper
⅔ cup dry red wine or beef stock or broth
1 cup water

* * * * *

1 teaspoon olive or vegetable oil

½ cup chopped onion
2 canned anchovy fillets, minced, optional
1 clove garlic, minced
½ cup chopped tomatoes
2 tablespoons tomato paste
1 tablespoon drained capers
½ teaspoon sugar
Salt
Pepper
2 tablespoons minced parsley

✿ Low Calorie
♥ Low Cholesterol
Servings: 4
Per Serving
Calories: 210
Fat: 5.7 g
Sodium: 52 mg
Cholesterol: 51 mg

Heat 1 tablespoon oil in pressure cooker over medium heat. Brown fish, about 30 seconds per side. Remove fish and sprinkle very lightly with garlic salt and pepper. Place greased cooking rack (or basket), wine, and water in pressure cooker. Place fish on rack (or in basket). Close cover securely. Place pressure regulator on vent pipe. COOK 2 MINUTES at 15 pounds pressure. Quick cool cooker. Remove fish, rack (or basket), and sauce and reserve, keeping fish warm. Heat 1 teaspoon oil in pressure cooker over medium heat. Sauté onion until tender. Add anchovies and garlic. Sauté 1 minute. Stir in reserved sauce, tomatoes, tomato paste, capers, and sugar. Cook over medium heat 3 minutes. Season to taste with salt and pepper. Stir in parsley. Spoon sauce over fish.

Intro

Basics

Appetizers

Soups and Stocks

Meats

Poultry

Seafood

Vegetables

Breads

Desserts

Whole Meal Magic

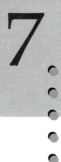

7. *Fish Spin Wheels*

3 flat fish fillets, Turbot, Sole, Flounder, Baby Salmon (about 1 pound)
2 medium carrots, cleaned and trimmed
1 small onion peel
1 celery rib, cleaned and trimmed
½ large red pepper, cleaned and seeded
1 cup champagne or dry white wine

½ cup water
1 tablespoon lemon juice
½ pound fresh spinach leaves, washed and torn
Salt
Pepper
2 teaspoons dillweed
1 teaspoon chopped parsley

½ cup cream or milk
1 tablespoon cornstarch
1 tablespoon cold water

❀ *Low Calorie*
❤ *Low Cholesterol*

Servings: 6
Per Serving
Calories: 142
Fat: 4.3 g
Sodium: 143 mg
Cholesterol: 7 mg

(Shown on page 155)

Cut fish fillets in half lengthwise. Roll and fasten with toothpicks. Cut carrots, onion, celery, and red pepper into julienne strips. Place rack (or basket), champagne, ½ cup water, and lemon juice in 6- or 8-quart pressure cooker. Pile spinach on rack (or in basket), pressing it down; arrange vegetables over spinach and sit fish roll-ups on vegetables. Sprinkle with salt, pepper, dillweed, and parsley. Close cover securely. Place pressure regulator on vent pipe. COOK 4 MINUTES at 15 pounds pressure. Quick cool cooker. Carefully lift out fish, vegetables, and rack (or basket). Keep warm. Add cream to cooker. Heat to boiling. Mix cornstarch with 1 tablespoon cold water; stir into cream mixture in cooker. Cook and stir until sauce boils and thickens. Serve fish on vegetables; spoon sauce over all.

Almond Cod with Peas

❀ *Low Calorie*
♥ *Low Cholesterol*

Servings: 4
Per Serving
Calories: 228
Fat: 6.4 g
Sodium: 227 mg
Cholesterol: 45 mg

(Shown on page 153)

1 **(1-pound) package frozen cod fillets**
½ **cup lightly packed parsley sprigs**
2 **tablespoons slivered or sliced almonds**
1 **tablespoon fresh oregano sprigs or ½ teaspoon dried oregano**
2 **large cloves garlic, cut into halves**
½ **teaspoon paprika**

1 **tablespoon vegetable oil**
½ **cup chicken stock or broth**
½ **cup dry white wine**
½ **cup water**

✳ ✳ ✳ ✳ ✳

1 **(10-ounce) package frozen peas**

✳ ✳ ✳ ✳ ✳

1 **tablespoon cornstarch, optional**
1 **tablespoon cold water, optional**

Let fish stand at room temperature while preparing herb mixture. Combine parsley, 1 tablespoon of the almonds, oregano, garlic, and paprika in food processor. Chop with on-and-off pulses. Heat oil in 6- or 8-quart pressure cooker over medium heat. Brown remaining 1 tablespoon almonds and remove. Drain on paper towels. Mix chicken stock, wine, and ½ cup water in pressure cooker. Stir in herb mixture. Place greased cooking rack (or basket) in pressure cooker. Cut fish into 4 even pieces. Place on rack (or in basket). Close cover securely. Place pressure regulator on vent pipe. COOK 2 MINUTES at 15 pounds pressure. Quick cool cooker. Remove fish and rack (or basket). Keep warm. Add frozen peas to cooking liquid. Close cover securely. Place pressure regulator on vent pipe. COOK 1 MINUTE at 15 pounds pressure. Quick cool cooker. If desired, mix cornstarch with 1 tablespoon cold water. Add to pea mixture. Cook and stir until mixture boils and thickens. Pour pea mixture into serving bowl. Top with fish. Sprinkle with toasted almonds.

Intro

Basics

Appetizers

Soups and Stocks

Meats

Poultry

Seafood

Vegetables

Breads

Desserts

Whole Meal Magic

Shrimp Pilau

- 1 cup long grain rice
- 1 (14½-ounce) can whole tomatoes, chopped
- 2 cloves garlic, minced
- 1 teaspoon sugar
- ½ cup chicken stock
- 1 teaspoon cider vinegar
- 2 cups water

* * * * *

- 2 slices bacon, diced
- ⅓ cup chopped onion
- ⅓ cup chopped green pepper
- 12 ounces shrimp, peeled, deveined

* * * * *

- Red pepper sauce
- Salt
- Pepper

✻ ***Low Calorie***

Servings: 4

Per Serving

Calories: 291

Fat: 3 g

Sodium: 467 mg

Cholesterol: 133 mg

Combine rice, tomatoes, garlic, sugar, chicken stock, and vinegar in metal bowl that fits loosely on rack (or in basket) in pressure cooker. Cover bowl securely with aluminum foil. Place water, cooking rack (or basket), and bowl in cooker. Close cover securely. Place pressure regulator on vent pipe. COOK 10 MINUTES at 15 pounds pressure. Let pressure drop of its own accord. Open cooker and allow rice to steam, uncovered, 5 minutes. Remove bowl, rack (or basket). Discard water. Fry bacon in pressure cooker over medium heat until crisp; remove bacon and reserve. Discard all but 1 tablespoon fat. Sauté onion and green pepper in fat until tender. Add shrimp; cook until shrimp are cooked through, about 3 minutes. Add rice mixture; cook until hot, about 2 minutes. Season to taste with red pepper sauce, salt, and pepper.

8 Vegetables and Side Dishes

> **"**...creatively prepared vegetables and side dishes have assumed star status.**"**

T hough we like to think of America as innovative, the rather ho-hum "meat and potatoes" approach to menu planning held sway in American cuisine for many years.

In the forties, fifties, and even sixties, it was the adventurous cook indeed who ventured very far from the accepted menu basics: meat and poultry entrée accompanied by a potato or white rice dish, a simple vegetable preparation and perhaps a green or fruit salad. While different entrée treatments came in and out of fashion during those decades, the side dishes that nestled next to the Chicken Kiev or Steak Diane or Chinese Pork Roast remained monotonously similar.

By the seventies, however, our culinary outlook had grown to encompass a more worldwide view of food, as well as its impact on our health and well-being. So, armed with our new appreciation for creativity and respect for nutrition, we were more than ready for the changes in the marketplace that would take place in the eighties. International food commerce suddenly brought hundreds of exotic ingredients from around the world right to our tables. There were new ones to discover every day and old ones to rediscover.

123

Provocative produce like broccoflower, fennel, kale, Jerusalem artichokes, and tomatillos entered the common cooking vocabulary. Root vegetables—turnips, rutabagas, parsnips, and beets—became popular once again.

Today, we have widened the definition of "side dishes," eagerly using all these marvelous ingredients to make them more substantial and filling. It's one way we compensate for the smaller meat and entrée portions on our plates, as we attempt to bring our diets in line with current nutritional guidelines. And we use lighter sauces and preparation styles to complement, not conceal, these simple, naturally-good foods.

The pressure cooker is a wonderful way to prepare all of these creative new meal components. Fresh vegetables, for example, retain more nutrients, as well as their natural colors and distinct flavors, because they cook in an almost airless environment and with very little liquid.

Root vegetables are especially easy to prepare in the pressure cooker too. The same beets that would take an hour to cook in a conventional pot, turn into tender, succulent eating in about 15 minutes!

Now that simple "meat and potatoes" is no longer the norm, creatively prepared vegetables and side dishes have assumed star status. With the following pressure cooker recipes, you'll get rave reviews, whether you're serving fresh *Ratatouille*, going ethnic with *Vegetable Antipasto* or accenting a roast with *Greek-Style Green Beans*.

Broccoflower with Cheddar Sauce

✿ Low Calorie
Servings: 6
Per Serving
Calories: 97
Fat: 5 g
Sodium: 175 mg
Cholesterol: 12 mg

1½ cups water
1 (1½-pound) head broccoflower
    or cauliflower
* * * * *
1 tablespoon margarine
1 tablespoon all-purpose flour
¾ cup milk

¼ cup finely diced pasteurized
    process cheese
¼ cup shredded Cheddar cheese
½ teaspoon prepared mustard
½ teaspoon prepared
    horseradish
    Dash red pepper sauce

Place cooking rack (or basket) and water in pressure cooker. Place broccoflower on rack (or in basket). Close cover securely. Place pressure regulator on vent pipe. COOK 2 TO 5 MINUTES at 15 pounds pressure. Quick cool cooker. Heat margarine in small saucepan over medium heat. Stir in flour. Cook over low heat 1 to 2 minutes. Stir in milk. Cook and stir until sauce boils and thickens. Remove pan from heat. Stir in cheeses until melted. Stir in mustard, horseradish, and pepper sauce. Spoon sauce over broccoflower.

● ● ● ● ● ● ●

Potato Salad

✿ Low Calorie
Servings: 12
Per Serving
Calories: 271
Fat: 14.9 g
Sodium: 327 mg
Cholesterol: 11 mg

(Shown on page 154)

2 cups water
4 pounds red-skinned potatoes
    (about 2½-inch diameter)
* * * * *
1 cup mayonnaise
¼ cup cider vinegar
2 tablespoons prepared mustard
1 teaspoon salt

½ teaspoon paprika
½ cup chopped celery
½ cup coarsely shredded carrot
½ cup finely chopped green
    pepper
¼ cup finely chopped onion
2 tablespoons chopped
    pimiento

Place cooking rack (or basket) and water in 6- or 8-quart pressure cooker. Place potatoes on rack (or in basket). Close cover securely. Place pressure regulator on vent pipe. COOK 15 MINUTES at 15 pounds pressure. Quick cool cooker. Cool, peel, and dice potatoes. Mix mayonnaise, vinegar, mustard, salt, and paprika. Toss potatoes, celery, carrot, green pepper, onion, and pimiento with mayonnaise dressing until mixed well. Pack into 9 x 5 x 3-inch loaf pan or shape by hand into loaf. Cover and refrigerate at least 2 hours or overnight. Unmold to serve. Cut into ¾-inch slices.

Vegetable Antipasto

1 cup water
½ cup white wine vinegar
2 cloves garlic, minced
1 teaspoon salt
1 teaspoon dried oregano
1 teaspoon freshly ground
  pepper
1 lemon, thinly sliced
2 carrots, cut into 3-inch sticks
1 green pepper, cut into rings
24 fresh green beans, cut into
  1-inch pieces

2 cups broccoli flowerettes
2 cups diagonally sliced celery
  (1-inch pieces)
2 bunches green onions, cut
  into 3-inch lengths

* * * * *

¾ cup olive oil
1 (7½-ounce) can water-packed
  tuna, optional

✿ Low Calorie

Servings: 10
Per Serving
Calories: 168
Fat: 16.4 g
Sodium: 245 mg
Cholesterol: 0

Combine water, vinegar, garlic, salt, oregano, and pepper in pressure cooker. Spread lemon slices on bottom of pressure cooker. Arrange vegetables in separate stacks on top of lemon. Do not fill pressure cooker over two-thirds full. Close cover securely. Place pressure regulator on vent pipe. COOK 0 MINUTES. Quick cool cooker. Remove vegetables in separate stacks to rectangular glass casserole. Repeat above procedure to cook any remaining vegetables. Discard lemon slices. Stir olive oil into cooking liquid; pour over vegetables. Refrigerate, covered, until chilled. Drain tuna and unmold in center of platter. Arrange drained vegetables around tuna. Spoon marinade over tuna.

✿ Low Calorie
♥ Low Cholesterol

Servings: 4
Per Serving
Calories: 102
Fat: 1.7 g
Sodium: 58 mg
Cholesterol: 0

Mashed Butternut Squash

1½ cups water
2 pound butternut squash,
  seeded, cut into quarters

* * * * *

1 tablespoon packed brown
  sugar

1 tablespoon margarine
2 teaspoons dry sherry,
  optional
1 teaspoon Dijon-style mustard
  Salt
  White pepper

Place cooking rack (or basket) and water in pressure cooker. Place squash on rack (or in basket). Close cover securely. Place pressure regulator on vent pipe. COOK 8 MINUTES at 15 pounds pressure. Quick cool cooker. Remove squash and rack (or basket) from pressure cooker. Discard water. When cool enough to handle, discard skin and mash squash with brown sugar, margarine, sherry, and mustard. Season to taste with salt and pepper. Return to pressure cooker. Cook over medium heat until hot.

Glazed New Potatoes with Herbs

1½ cups chicken stock or broth
     or water
1   pound small new potatoes
     (about 12)

* * * * *

¼   cup margarine, divided

2   tablespoons sugar
1   teaspoon balsamic or red wine
     vinegar
½   teaspoon dried mint
½   teaspoon dried oregano

Place cooking rack (or basket) and chicken stock in pressure cooker. Place potatoes on rack (or in basket). Close cover securely. Place pressure regulator on vent pipe. COOK 5 MINUTES at 15 pounds pressure. Quick cool cooker. Remove potatoes and rack (or basket). Discard stock. Heat 2 tablespoons of the margarine in the pressure cooker over medium heat. Stir in sugar. Cook and stir until sugar has melted and browned, about 1 minute. Remove from heat. Stir in remaining 2 tablespoons margarine, vinegar, mint, and oregano. Add potatoes. Toss to coat.

Hopping John

1   cup dried black eyed peas
¼   cup vegetable oil
1½ teaspoons salt
     Water to cover peas
3   slices bacon, diced
½   cup chopped onion
½   cup chopped green pepper

½   cup chopped celery
2   cups chicken stock
½   teaspoon crushed red pepper

* * * * *

1½ cups cooked rice
     Red pepper sauce
     Salt

Soak peas overnight in oil, salt, and water to cover; drain. Fry bacon in pressure cooker over medium heat until crisp. Remove bacon and reserve. Drain all but 1 tablespoon fat from pressure cooker. Add onion, green pepper, and celery to pressure cooker. Sauté until tender. Stir in chicken stock, red pepper, and peas. Close cover securely. Place pressure regulator on vent pipe. COOK 8 MINUTES at 15 pounds pressure. Let pressure drop of its own accord. Stir in rice; season to taste with red pepper sauce and salt. Stir in reserved bacon.

Intro

Basics

Appetizers

Soups
and
Stocks

Meats

Poultry

Seafood

Vegetables

Breads

Desserts

Whole
Meal
Magic

Sunchokes Au Gratin

20 ounces fresh sunchokes (Jerusalem artichokes)*
1½ cups water
4 teaspoons lemon juice

* * * * *

2 (3-ounce) packages cream cheese, softened

¼ cup butter
¼ cup shredded Parmesan cheese
Pinch pepper
1 teaspoon grated Parmesan cheese
Paprika

 **Low Calorie**
Servings: 8
Per Serving
Calories: 194
Fat: 14.2 g
Sodium: 188 mg
Cholesterol: 42 mg

Combine sunchokes, water, and lemon juice in pressure cooker. Close cover securely. Place pressure regulator on vent pipe. COOK 3 MINUTES at 15 pounds pressure. Quick cool cooker. Remove sunchokes and cool slightly. Reserve ½ cup cooking liquid. Peel and slice or dice sunchokes. Place in buttered au gratin dish. Mix cream cheese, butter, shredded cheese, and pepper. Whisk in ½ cup reserved hot liquid. Pour over sunchokes. Sprinkle with grated cheese and paprika. Broil for 3 or 4 minutes or until top is browned.

*Other washed and peeled root vegetables, such as carrots or turnips, can be substituted for sunchokes. Refer to pressure cooker instruction manual for cooking times.

● ● ● ● ● ● ●

 Low Calorie
Low Cholesterol
Servings: 6
Per Serving
Calories: 58
Fat: 0
Sodium: 80 mg
Cholesterol: 0

(Shown on page 145)

Fruit and Beets

4 whole fresh beets with tops (2½-inch diameter)
2 cups water

* * * * *

2 teaspoons lemon juice

¼ cup natural apricot or orange fruit spread
Pinch salt
Pinch ground nutmeg

Cut off all but 2 inches of beet tops. Scrub beets thoroughly. Place beets and water in 6- or 8-quart pressure cooker. Close cover securely. Place pressure regulator on vent pipe. COOK 15 MINUTES at 15 pounds pressure. Quick cool cooker. Drain beets. Rinse under cold water and slip off skins. Cut beets into cubes or slices. Combine lemon juice, fruit spread, salt, and nutmeg in pressure cooker. Heat and stir to soften spread. Stir in beets and heat.

Vegetable Risotto

❁ *Low Calorie*
❤ *Low Cholesterol*
Servings: 6
Per Serving
Calories: 230
Fat: 7.5 g
Sodium: 394 mg
Cholesterol: 3 mg

¼ ounce dried Italian mushrooms
Hot water
1 tablespoon olive or vegetable oil
1 cup chopped onion
1 cup coarsely chopped yellow summer squash
½ teaspoon dried Italian herbs

1 cup Arborio rice
2⅓ cups chicken stock
1½ cups water

* * * * *

½ cup frozen peas, thawed
¼ cup toasted pine nuts
¼ cup grated Parmesan cheese
Salt
Pepper

Soak dried mushrooms in hot water until soft, about 10 minutes; drain and chop. Heat oil in pressure cooker over medium heat. Sauté mushrooms, onion, squash, and herbs until onion is tender; remove from pressure cooker and reserve. Combine rice and chicken stock in metal bowl that fits loosely on rack (or in basket) in pressure cooker. Cover bowl securely with aluminum foil. Place 1½ cups water, cooking rack (or basket), and bowl in cooker. Close cover securely. Place pressure regulator on vent pipe. COOK 8 MINUTES at 15 pounds pressure. Quick cool cooker. Stir reserved sautéed vegetables, peas, nuts, and cheese into rice. Season to taste with salt and pepper.

NOTE: Arborio rice can be purchased in Italian groceries and in specialty departments in large supermarkets. Regular rice can be substituted in the recipe, but the risotto will not be as creamy in texture.

• • • • • • •

Lemoned Broccoli

❁ *Low Calorie*
❤ *Low Cholesterol*
Servings: 6
Per Serving
Calories: 42
Fat: 0.5 g
Sodium: 39 mg
Cholesterol: 0

2 pounds broccoli
1½ cups water
Salt

Pepper
4 thin slices lemon

Trim off large leaves and tough ends of broccoli stalks. Score ends. Place cooking rack (or basket) and water in 6- or 8-quart pressure cooker. Place broccoli on rack (or in basket). Sprinkle broccoli with salt and pepper. Top with lemon slices. Close cover securely. Place pressure regulator on vent pipe. COOK 1 TO 2 MINUTES at 15 pounds pressure. Quick cool cooker.

Intro

Basics

Appetizers

Soups and Stocks

Meats

Poultry

Seafood

Vegetables

Breads

Desserts

Whole Meal Magic

Wild Rice

1 cup wild rice
2 cups water

2½ cups water

Combine rice and 2 cups water in metal bowl that fits loosely on rack (or in basket) in pressure cooker. Cover bowl securely with aluminum foil. Place cooking rack (or basket) and 2½ cups water in pressure cooker. Place bowl on rack (or in basket). Close cover securely. Place pressure regulator on vent pipe. COOK 20 MINUTES (al dente or crunchy rice) OR 25 MINUTES (softer rice), at 15 pounds pressure. Let pressure drop of its own accord. Open pressure cooker and let rice steam, uncovered, 5 minutes.

Brown Rice

1 cup natural brown rice
1½ cups water

2 cups water

Combine rice and 1½ cups water in metal bowl that fits loosely on rack (or in basket) in pressure cooker. Cover bowl securely with aluminum foil. Place cooking rack (or basket) and 2 cups water in pressure cooker. Place bowl on rack (or in basket). Close cover securely. Place pressure regulator on vent pipe. COOK 10 MINUTES at 15 pounds pressure. Let pressure drop of its own accord. Open pressure cooker and let rice steam, uncovered, 5 minutes.

Steamed Rice

1 cup long grain white rice
1½ cups water

2 cups water

Combine rice and 1½ cups water in metal bowl that fits loosely on rack (or in basket) in pressure cooker. Cover bowl securely with aluminum foil. Place cooking rack (or basket) and 2 cups water in pressure cooker. Place bowl on rack (or in basket). Close cover securely. Place pressure regulator on vent pipe. COOK 5 MINUTES at 15 pounds pressure. Let pressure drop of its own accord. Open pressure cooker and let rice steam, uncovered, 5 minutes.

Mexican Black Beans

♣ *Low Calorie*
♥ *Low Cholesterol*

Servings: 6
Per Serving
Calories: 186
Fat: 5.7 g
Sodium: 741 mg
Cholesterol: 0

1½ cups dried black beans	1 bay leaf
3 tablespoons vegetable oil	1 cup chopped tomato
2 teaspoons salt	2-3 teaspoons minced jalapeño chile
Water to cover beans	
1 tablespoon olive or vegetable oil	1 tablespoon all-purpose flour
	½ teaspoon salt
¾ cup finely chopped onion	¼ teaspoon ground cumin
2 cloves garlic, minced	2½ cups beef stock or broth

Soak beans overnight in 3 tablespoons oil, 2 teaspoons salt, and water to cover; drain. Heat oil in pressure cooker over medium heat. Sauté onion, garlic, and bay leaf 2 minutes. Stir in tomato, chile, flour, ½ teaspoon salt, and cumin. Sauté 2 minutes. Add beans and beef stock. Close cover securely. Place pressure regulator on vent pipe. COOK 35 MINUTES at 15 pounds pressure. Let pressure drop of its own accord.

Curried Carrots

♣ *Low Calorie*
Servings: 4
Per Serving
Calories: 156
Fat: 8.1 g
Sodium: 186 mg
Cholesterol: 15 mg

(Shown on page 147)

12 ounces mini carrots or cut-up large carrots, pared	1 tablespoon orange marmalade or apple jelly
½ cup beef stock or broth	* * * * *
1 cup water	1 tablespoon water
2 tablespoons minced onion	1-2 teaspoons curry powder
2 tablespoons butter	1 teaspoon all-purpose flour
2 tablespoons sliced almonds or shredded coconut	1 banana, sliced

Combine carrots, beef stock, water, onion, butter, almonds, and marmalade in pressure cooker. Close cover securely. Place pressure regulator on vent pipe. COOK 2 MINUTES at 15 pounds pressure. Quick cool cooker. Push carrots to one side of pressure cooker. Mix water, curry powder, and flour. Add curry mixture to liquid in pressure cooker. Cook and stir until liquid boils and thickens. Gently stir in banana. Serve at once.

Intro

Basics

Appetizers

Soups and Stocks

Meats

Poultry

Seafood

Vegetables

Breads

Desserts

Whole Meal Magic

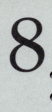

Parsnip Salad

2 pounds parsnips or parsley root
1½ cups water

* * * * *

⅓ cup olive oil

2 tablespoons lemon juice
1 teaspoon minced parsley
⅛ teaspoon salt
3-4 drops red pepper sauce
Pinch pepper

Place parsnips in pressure cooker, cutting to fit if necessary. Add water. Close cover securely. Place pressure regulator on vent pipe. COOK 2-INCH PARSNIPS 10 MINUTES, 1- TO 1½-INCH PARSNIPS 8 MINUTES AND SMALLER PARSNIPS 5 MINUTES at 15 pounds pressure. Quick cool cooker. Remove parsnips and cool slightly. Remove skins. Cut into 3-inch lengths and then into sticks. Remove cores if stringy. Place parsnips in bowl. Mix remaining ingredients. Pour over parsnips. Serve at room temperature.

NOTE: *The English call this Poor Man's Lobster Salad when served on lettuce with hard-cooked eggs, cucumber, cherry tomatoes, and mayonnaise.*

Garden Vegetable Salad

1½ cups water
2 cups cauliflower flowerettes
2 cups broccoli flowerettes
2 cups green beans

* * * * *

1 cup sliced mushrooms

1 cup diced celery
1 (8-ounce) bottle buttermilk-based salad dressing
8 lettuce leaves
Danish blue cheese, crumbled
4-5 Red radishes

Place cooking rack (or basket) and water in 6- or 8-quart pressure cooker. Place cauliflower, broccoli, and beans on rack (or in basket). Close cover securely. Place pressure regulator on vent pipe. COOK 0 MINUTES. Quick cool cooker. Drain vegetables. Toss with mushrooms, celery, and dressing. Place salad in lettuce-lined bowl. Serve at room temperature or chilled. Garnish with cheese and radishes.

Red Hot Pintos

1½ cups dried pinto beans
3 tablespoons vegetable oil
2 teaspoons salt
   Cold water to cover beans
1 tablespoon vegetable oil
1 cup chopped green onion
1-2 jalapeño chilies, seeded, deveined, minced
1 clove garlic, minced

1 tablespoon all-purpose flour
½ teaspoon chili powder
½ teaspoon paprika
¼ teaspoon ground cumin
3 cups water
1 smoked ham hock

* * * * *

Salt
Pepper

❀ *Low Calorie*
❤ *Low Cholesterol*
Servings: 8
Per Serving
Calories: 130
Fat: 4 g
Sodium: 491 mg
Cholesterol: 2 mg

Soak beans overnight in 3 tablespoons oil, 2 teaspoons salt, and cold water to cover; drain. Heat 1 tablespoon oil in pressure cooker over medium heat. Sauté green onion, chilies, and garlic until tender. Stir in flour, chili powder, paprika, and cumin. Sauté 1 minute. Add beans, 3 cups water, and ham hock. Close cover securely. Place pressure regulator on vent pipe. COOK 25 MINUTES at 15 pounds pressure. Let pressure drop of its own accord. If desired, simmer briskly, uncovered, to reduce liquid. Season to taste with salt and pepper.

● ● ● ● ● ● ●

Greek-Style Green Beans

1 tablespoon olive or vegetable oil
½ cup chopped onion
3 large cloves garlic, minced
1 pound whole green beans

3 cups chopped tomatoes
1 cup water

* * * * *

Salt
Pepper

❀ *Low Calorie*
Servings: 8
Per Serving
Calories: 51
Fat: 2 g
Sodium: 6 mg
Cholesterol: 0

Heat oil in pressure cooker over medium heat. Sauté onion and garlic until tender. Stir in green beans, tomatoes, and water. Close cover securely. Place pressure regulator on vent pipe. COOK 2 MINUTES at 15 pounds pressure. Quick cool cooker. Season to taste with salt and pepper.

Intro

Basics

Appetizers

Soups and Stocks

Meats

Poultry

Seafood

Vegetables

Breads

Desserts

Whole Meal Magic

Savory Mushroom Bread Pudding

1 tablespoon margarine	⅛ teaspoon pepper
4 ounces mushrooms, sliced	3 slices firm white bread,
¼ cup chopped onion	lightly buttered, cubed
¼ cup chopped red or green	(2 cups)
pepper	¾ cup milk
¼ cup chopped celery	2 eggs
¼ cup mayonnaise	¼ cup shredded Cheddar cheese
½ teaspoon salt	3 cups water

❀ *Low Calorie*

Servings: 8

Per Serving
Calories: 133
Fat: 9.8 g
Sodium: 294 mg
Cholesterol: 63 mg

Heat margarine in pressure cooker over medium heat. Sauté mushrooms until tender. Remove from heat. Stir in onion, red pepper, celery, mayonnaise, salt, and pepper. Layer half the bread in greased 1-quart casserole that fits loosely on rack (or in basket) in pressure cooker. Top with half the mushroom mixture. Repeat layers. Beat milk and eggs. Pour over top. Sprinkle with cheese. Cover casserole securely with aluminum foil. Place cooking rack (or basket) and water in pressure cooker. Place casserole on rack (or in basket). Close cover securely. Do not place pressure regulator on vent pipe. COOK 10 MINUTES with steam flowing very gently through vent pipe. Place pressure regulator on vent pipe. COOK 5 MINUTES at 15 pounds pressure. Quick cool cooker. Let stand 5 minutes before serving.

Wild and White Rice with Cashews

❀ *Low Calorie*

Servings: 6

Per Serving
Calories: 234
Fat: 9.7 g
Sodium: 525 mg
Cholesterol: 12 mg

2 tablespoons margarine	1 teaspoon Worcestershire sauce
2 cups sliced mushrooms	½ teaspoon salt
¼ cup chopped onion	⅛ teaspoon pepper
1 (6¼-ounce) package long	2 cups water
grain and wild rice (spice	* * * * *
packets discarded)	⅔ cup shredded Swiss cheese
2 cups beef stock	⅓ cup cashews

Heat margarine in 6- or 8-quart pressure cooker over medium heat. Sauté mushrooms and onion until tender; stir in rice, beef stock, Worcestershire sauce, salt, and pepper. Transfer mixture to metal bowl that fits loosely on rack (or in basket) in pressure cooker. Cover bowl securely with aluminum foil. Place water, cooking rack (or basket), and bowl in cooker. Close cover securely. Place pressure regulator on vent pipe. COOK 10 MINUTES at 15 pounds pressure. Let pressure drop of its own accord. Stir in cheese and cashews.

Sweet Potatoes and Apple Rings

1½ cups water
3 medium sweet potatoes, 1½ pounds, pared, cut into quarters

* * * * *

4 tablespoons butter
3 tablespoons honey
¼ teaspoon ground cloves
¼ teaspoon ground cinnamon
Salt
Pepper
2 tablespoons butter
1 cooking apple, cored, cut into 6 rings

❀ *Low Calorie*
Servings: 6
Per Serving
Calories: 237
Fat: 11.6 g
Sodium: 126 mg
Cholesterol: 31 mg

Place cooking rack (or basket) and water in pressure cooker. Place sweet potatoes on rack (or in basket). Close cover securely. Place pressure regulator on vent pipe. COOK 8 MINUTES at 15 pounds pressure. Quick cool cooker. Mash sweet potatoes, or process in food processor, with 4 tablespoons butter, honey, cloves, cinnamon, salt, and pepper to taste. Keep warm. Heat 2 tablespoons butter in skillet over medium heat. Sauté apple rings until tender. Spoon sweet potatoes, or pipe through pastry bag, onto apple rings.

● ● ● ● ● ●

Beans and Sausage

1 pound dried pinto beans
¼ cup vegetable oil
1 tablespoon salt
Water to cover beans
1 pound bulk pork sausage
1 cup chopped onion
4 cups water
1 (8-ounce) can tomato sauce
¼ cup packed brown sugar
¼ cup light molasses
2 tablespoons paprika
1 tablespoon chili powder
1 teaspoon salt
1 teaspoon dry mustard

Servings: 8
Per Serving
Calories: 437
Fat: 17.1 g
Sodium: 1298 mg
Cholesterol: 37 mg

Soak beans overnight in oil, 1 tablespoon salt, and water to cover; drain. Crumble and brown sausage in 6- or 8-quart pressure cooker over medium heat. Remove sausage. Discard all but 1 tablespoon fat. Sauté onion until tender. Stir in sausage, beans, and remaining ingredients. Close cover securely. Place pressure regulator on vent pipe. COOK 25 MINUTES at 15 pounds pressure. Let pressure drop of its own accord. Remove cover and simmer to desired consistency.

Intro

Basics

Appetizers

Soups and Stocks

Meats

Poultry

Seafood

Vegetables

Breads

Desserts

Whole Meal Magic

135

Braised Kale

✤ *Low Calorie*

Servings: 4
Per Serving
Calories: 53
Fat: 1.8 g
Sodium: 75 mg
Cholesterol: 3 mg

2 slices bacon, diced
½ cup chopped onion
1 clove garlic, minced
½ pound kale, torn into bite-size pieces

1½ cups water

* * * * *

¼ cup plain nonfat yogurt
Salt
Pepper

Fry bacon in pressure cooker over medium heat until crisp. Remove bacon and reserve. Discard all but 1 tablespoon fat. Add onion and garlic. Sauté until tender. Remove onion mixture and reserve. Add kale and water to pressure cooker. Close cover securely. Place pressure regulator on vent pipe. COOK 0 MINUTES. Quick cool cooker. Drain excess water from pressure cooker. Stir yogurt, reserved onion mixture, and bacon into kale. Season to taste with salt and pepper.

● ● ● ● ● ● ●

✤ *Low Calorie*

Servings: 8
Per Serving
Calories: 224
Fat: 11.1 g
Sodium: 656 mg
Cholesterol: 71 mg

Tex-Mex Corn Pudding

1 (8½-ounce) package corn bread mix
1 cup frozen (thawed) or canned whole kernel corn, drained
⅔ cup milk
⅔ cup sour cream
½ cup shredded Colby cheese
2 eggs, beaten
¼ cup chopped red pepper

¼ cup chopped onion
½ (4-ounce) can hot or mild green chilies, drained, chopped
1 teaspoon chili powder
¼ teaspoon red pepper sauce
¼ teaspoon salt
3½ cups water

Combine corn bread mix with remaining ingredients except water. Mix well. Spoon into 1-quart soufflé dish or casserole that fits on rack (or in basket) in pressure cooker. Cover dish securely with aluminum foil. Place cooking rack (or basket) and water in pressure cooker. Place soufflé dish on rack (or in basket). Close cover securely. Do not place pressure regulator on vent pipe. COOK 5 MINUTES with steam flowing very gently through vent pipe. Place pressure regulator on vent pipe. COOK 25 MINUTES at 15 pounds pressure. Let pressure drop of its own accord.

Turnip Timbales

1 pound turnips, pared, diced
(1-inch pieces)
1½ cups water
1 teaspoon sugar
½ teaspoon salt
1 carrot, pared, thinly sliced

* * * * *

2 tablespoons all-purpose flour

½ cup sour cream
2 eggs
¼-½ teaspoon salt
¼ teaspoon white pepper
⅛ teaspoon ground nutmeg
1½ cups water

* * * * *

Hollandaise sauce, optional

✿ *Low Calorie*
Servings: 5
Per Serving
Calories: 115
Fat: 7 g
Sodium: 405 mg
Cholesterol: 95 mg

(Shown on page 147)

Combine turnips, 1½ cups water, sugar, and ½ teaspoon salt in 6- or 8-quart pressure cooker. Wrap carrot securely in aluminum foil packet. Place on top of turnips. Close cover securely. Place pressure regulator on vent pipe. COOK 4 MINUTES at 15 pounds pressure. Quick cool cooker. Arrange carrot slices in bottom of 4 or 5 buttered timbale molds or custard cups that fit loosely on rack (or in basket) in pressure cooker. Drain turnips thoroughly. Purée in food processor or blender. Add flour and process. Add sour cream and process. With processor running, add eggs, one at a time. Add remaining salt, pepper, and nutmeg. Pour purée over carrots in molds. Tap molds on counter to settle. Cover molds securely with aluminum foil. Place cooking rack (or basket) and 1½ cups water in pressure cooker. Place molds on rack (or in basket), adding another rack for a second layer if necessary. Close cover securely. Place pressure regulator on vent pipe. COOK 5 MINUTES at 15 pounds pressure. Quick cool cooker. Remove timbales and let cool in molds on wire rack 10 minutes. Loosen edges and unmold. Serve with hollandaise sauce, if desired.

● ● ● ● ● ● ●

Leeks with Mushrooms

1 tablespoon margarine
2 cups julienne-cut leeks
(white parts only)
2 cups medium mushroom
caps (about 6 ounces)

¾ cup beef stock or broth
¾ cup water

* * * * *

Salt
Pepper

✿ *Low Calorie*
♥ *Low Cholesterol*
Servings: 6
Per Serving
Calories: 45
Fat: 1.4 g
Sodium: 128 mg
Cholesterol: 0

Heat margarine in pressure cooker over medium heat. Sauté leeks and mushrooms until tender, about 2 minutes. Add beef stock and water. Close cover securely. Place pressure regulator on vent pipe. COOK 1 MINUTE at 15 pounds pressure. Quick cool cooker. Season to taste with salt and pepper.

Intro

Basics

Appetizers

Soups
and
Stocks

Meats

Poultry

Seafood

Vegetables

Breads

Desserts

Whole
Meal
Magic

Vegetables Vinaigrette

2 cups assorted julienne-cut
  fresh vegetables, such as
  green beans, carrots, turnips,
  celery, and green pepper
1 tablespoon butter
1½ cups water

⁕ ⁕ ⁕ ⁕ ⁕

⅓ cup olive oil
4 teaspoons white wine vinegar
¼ teaspoon dry mustard
¼ teaspoon salt
  Pinch pepper

❀ Low Calorie

Servings: 4
Per Serving
Calories: 207
Fat: 21 g
Sodium: 173 mg
Cholesterol: 8 mg

Wrap vegetables with butter securely in aluminum foil packet. Place cooking rack (or basket) and water in pressure cooker. Place vegetable packet on rack (or in basket). Close cover securely. Place pressure regulator on vent pipe. COOK 5 MINUTES at 15 pounds pressure. Quick cool cooker. Remove vegetables from packet. Place in bowl. Mix oil, vinegar, mustard, salt, and pepper. Pour over vegetables and toss. Refrigerate, covered, several hours or overnight.

● ● ● ● ● ● ●

❀ Low Calorie
♥ Low Cholesterol

Servings: 6
Per Serving
Calories: 221
Fat: 7.4 g
Sodium: 117 mg
Cholesterol: 19 mg

Middle East Brown Rice

1 cup brown rice
1½ cups beef broth
2 cups water

⁕ ⁕ ⁕ ⁕ ⁕

½-1 pound lean lamb, beef, or pork
2 tablespoons olive oil
1 medium onion, chopped
2 tablespoons lemon juice
¾ cup beef broth

¾ cup water
¼ teaspoon pepper

⁕ ⁕ ⁕ ⁕ ⁕

½ pound mushrooms, sliced
2 tablespoons crushed dried
  mint or chopped fresh mint
2 tablespoons chopped parsley
  Yogurt

Combine rice and 1½ cups beef broth in metal bowl that fits loosely on rack (or in basket) in pressure cooker. Cover bowl securely with aluminum foil. Place cooking rack (or basket) and water in pressure cooker. Place bowl on rack (or in basket). Close cover securely. Place pressure regulator on vent pipe. COOK 10 MINUTES at 15 pounds pressure. Let pressure drop of its own accord. Open pressure cooker and let rice steam, uncovered, 5 minutes. Remove bowl, cooking rack (or basket), and water. Trim fat from meat if necessary, cut into small cubes. Heat oil in pressure cooker over medium heat and brown meat; add onion and cook until soft. Add lemon juice, ¾ cup beef broth, ¾ cup water, and pepper. Close cover securely. Place pressure regulator on vent pipe. COOK 8 MINUTES at 15 pounds pressure. Quick cool cooker. Add sliced mushrooms, rice, mint, and parsley; cook for a few minutes stirring constantly. Serve in bowls with yogurt.

Ratatouille

2 cups cubed pared eggplant
  Salt
2-3 tablespoons olive or
  vegetable oil
1½ cups chopped red or green
  peppers
1½ cups chopped onions
½ cup sliced celery
2-3 cloves garlic, minced
1½ cups sliced zucchini
1 teaspoon dried thyme

½ teaspoon dried rosemary
½ teaspoon dried marjoram
1 bay leaf
2 cups chopped tomatoes
¾ cup water
½ cup white wine
* * * * *
2 tablespoons tomato paste
  Salt
  Pepper

❀ *Low Calorie*
Servings: 8
Per Serving
Calories: 82
Fat: 3.7 g
Sodium: 45 mg
Cholesterol: 0

Spread eggplant on paper towels. Sprinkle lightly with salt and let stand 20 minutes. Rinse and drain. Press out excess liquid with clean paper towels. Heat oil in 6- or 8-quart pressure cooker over medium heat. Sauté red peppers, onions, celery, and garlic until tender. Add eggplant, zucchini, and herbs. Sauté 3 minutes. Stir in tomatoes, water, and wine. Close cover securely. Place pressure regulator on vent pipe. COOK 3 MINUTES at 15 pounds pressure. Quick cool cooker. Stir in tomato paste and simmer to thicken. Season to taste with salt and pepper. Serve hot or cold.

● ● ● ● ● ● ●

Savory Swedes

1 rutabaga, about 1½ pounds
1 large white potato, about 1
  pound
1½ cups water
1 teaspoon sugar
½ teaspoon salt

* * * * *
1 tablespoon minced onion
3 tablespoons butter
¼ cup milk
½ cup shredded Cheddar cheese

❀ *Low Calorie*
Servings: 5
Per Serving
Calories: 224
Fat: 11.1 g
Sodium: 380 mg
Cholesterol: 31 mg

(Shown on page 147)

Pare rutabaga and potato and cut into 1-inch cubes (about 6 cups). Combine in 6- or 8-quart pressure cooker with water, sugar, and salt. Close cover securely. Place pressure regulator on vent pipe. COOK 3 MINUTES at 15 pounds pressure. Quick cool cooker. Drain rutabaga and potato thoroughly. Mash or whip until smooth and fluffy. Cook onion slowly in butter over medium heat until tender. Add milk and heat. Beat into rutabaga mixture. Beat in cheese. Serve as is, or spoon into 1-quart casserole, top with additional cheese and bake in 325 degree F oven to melt cheese.

Intro

Basics

Appetizers

Soups
and
Stocks

Meats

Poultry

Seafood

Vegetables

Breads

Desserts

Whole
Meal
Magic

Garlic Pumpkin with Yogurt Sauce

1 small pumpkin or 1 medium acorn or butternut squash	¼ teaspoon paprika
¾ cup dry white wine	⅛ teaspoon pepper
1¼ cups water	2-4 drops red pepper sauce
2 tablespoons packed brown sugar	* * * * *
8 small to medium cloves garlic	1 cup plain yogurt
½ teaspoon salt	1 tablespoon lemon juice
	¼ teaspoon salt

❋ *Low Calorie*
♥ *Low Cholesterol*

Servings: 4
Per Serving
Calories: 136
Fat: 1.1 g
Sodium: 445 mg
Cholesterol: 3 mg

Cut pumpkin into quarters. Discard seeds. Combine wine, water, brown sugar, garlic, ½ teaspoon salt, paprika, pepper, and pepper sauce in pressure cooker. Place cooking rack (or basket) in pressure cooker. Place pumpkin, cut sides down, on rack (or in basket). Close cover securely. Place pressure regulator on vent pipe. COOK 12 MINUTES at 15 pounds pressure. Quick cool cooker. Remove pumpkin and rack (or basket). Cool slightly. Remove pumpkin skin. Mash garlic into cooking liquid. Pour over pumpkin. Mix yogurt, lemon juice, and ¼ teaspoon salt. Serve sauce with hot or room temperature pumpkin.

● ● ● ● ● ● ●

Roots with Ginger Sauce

❋ *Low Calorie*
♥ *Low Cholesterol*

Servings: 6
Per Serving
Calories: 60
Fat: 1.3 g
Sodium: 232 mg
Cholesterol: 0

(Shown on page 64)

1 (10-ounce) package baby carrots or 4 medium carrots, cut into chunks	1 tablespoon sugar
	1 tablespoon low cholesterol margarine
3-4 small turnips	⅛ teaspoon salt
1 cup chicken broth	Dash pepper
½ cup water	* * * * *
1-2 tablespoons minced fresh gingerroot or ½ teaspoon ground ginger	2 tablespoons cornstarch
	2 tablespoons cold water

Scrub or peel carrots, trimming ends. Pare turnips and cut into sixths. Put chicken broth, ½ cup water, gingerroot, sugar, margarine, salt, and pepper in pressure cooker. Put rack (or basket) in cooker. Place vegetables on rack (or in basket). Close cover securely. Place pressure regulator on vent pipe. COOK 6 MINUTES at 15 pounds pressure. Quick cool cooker. Remove vegetables. Blend cornstarch into 2 tablespoons cold water; stir into hot liquid. Cook and stir until mixture thickens. Put vegetables in sauce and stir to coat.

Brown Rice with Veggies

1 cup natural brown rice
1½ cups chicken stock or broth
1 (2-ounce) package sliced blanched almonds
1 large tomato, peeled, seeded, chopped
½ cup diced carrot
½ cup diced celery
½ cup diced green pepper
½ cup sliced green onion
2 cups water

* * * * *

¼ cup chopped parsley

❀ *Low Calorie*
♥ *Low Cholesterol*
Servings: 4
Per Serving
Calories: 290
Fat: 9.5 g
Sodium: 319 mg
Cholesterol: 0

(Shown on page 55)

Combine rice and chicken stock in metal bowl that fits loosely on rack (or in basket) in 6- or 8-quart pressure cooker. Stir in almonds and vegetables. Cover bowl securely with aluminum foil. Place cooking rack (or basket) and water in pressure cooker. Place bowl on rack (or in basket). Close cover securely. Place pressure regulator on vent pipe. COOK 10 MINUTES at 15 pounds pressure. Let pressure drop of its own accord. Open pressure cooker and let rice steam, uncovered, 10 minutes. Stir in parsley.

● ● ● ● ● ● ●

German Potato Salad

3 slices bacon, diced
⅓ cup chopped onion
¼ cup chopped green pepper
3 tablespoons distilled white vinegar
2 tablespoons sugar
1 teaspoon Dijon-style mustard
Dash red pepper sauce
Salt
Pepper
1½ cups chicken stock or broth or water
1 pound red-skinned potatoes, unpared, cut into quarters

❀ *Low Calorie*
♥ *Low Cholesterol*
Servings: 4
Per Serving
Calories: 167
Fat: 2.9 g
Sodium: 292 mg
Cholesterol: 4 mg

Fry bacon in pressure cooker over medium heat until crisp. Remove bacon and reserve. Discard all but 1 tablespoon fat. Add onion and green pepper. Sauté until tender. Stir in vinegar, sugar, mustard, and pepper sauce. Season to taste with salt and pepper. Remove dressing from pressure cooker and reserve. Place cooking rack (or basket) and chicken stock in pressure cooker. Place potatoes on rack (or in basket). Close cover securely. Place pressure regulator on vent pipe. COOK 3 MINUTES at 15 pounds pressure. Quick cool cooker. Discard stock. Toss potatoes with reserved dressing and bacon.

Intro

Basics

Appetizers

Soups
and
Stocks

Meats

Poultry

Seafood

Vegetables

Breads

Desserts

Whole
Meal
Magic

Ginger-Orange Carrots

1 pound carrots, cut lengthwise into quarters	½ cup butter, melted
½ cup frozen orange juice concentrate, thawed	1 tablespoon honey
1½ cups water	½ teaspoon ground ginger
	½ teaspoon salt

Servings: 4
Per Serving
Calories: 321
Fat: 23.1 g
Sodium: 540 mg
Cholesterol: 61 mg

Place carrots in pressure cooker. Mix remaining ingredients. Pour over carrots. Close cover securely. Place pressure regulator on vent pipe. COOK 3 MINUTES at 15 pounds pressure. Quick cool cooker.

Savory Rice Stuffed Onions

❣ *Low Calorie*
♥ *Low Cholesterol*
Servings: 4
Per Serving
Calories: 235
Fat: 5.3 g
Sodium: 347 mg
Cholesterol: 53 mg

(Shown on page 57)

4 medium sweet Spanish onions, (9 to 10 ounces each)	¼ teaspoon minced fresh gingerroot
1½ teaspoons vegetable oil	1 cup cooked rice
1 egg, slightly beaten	¼ (10-ounce) package frozen peas
1½ teaspoons vegetable oil	1 tablespoon soy sauce
¼ cup thinly sliced celery	1½ cups water
¼ teaspoon minced garlic	

Remove skins and slice ½ inch from top of each onion. Scoop out centers of onions leaving ½ inch, about 3 rings. Chop enough onion centers to make 2 tablespoons. Heat 1½ teaspoons oil in 6- or 8-quart pressure cooker over medium heat; add egg and scramble. Remove from cooker and set aside. Heat remaining 1½ teaspoons oil in cooker. Add chopped onion, celery, garlic, and gingerroot; stir-fry 1 minute. Add cooked rice, egg, peas, and soy sauce. Stir-fry 1 minute. Remove from heat and spoon into onion shells. Place water and cooking rack (or basket) in pressure cooker. Place onions on rack (or in basket). Close cover securely. Place pressure regulator on vent pipe. COOK 8 MINUTES at 15 pounds pressure. Quick cool cooker.

Lemon Rice

❀ *Low Calorie*
♥ *Low Cholesterol*

Servings: 4
Per Serving
Calories: 183
Fat: 0.8 g
Sodium: 693 mg
Cholesterol: 0

1 cup long grain rice	2 cups water
1½ cups chicken stock	* * * * *
2 teaspoons lemon juice	1 teaspoon grated lemon rind
¾ teaspoon salt	

Combine rice, stock, lemon juice, and salt in metal bowl that fits loosely on rack (or in basket) in pressure cooker. Cover bowl securely with aluminum foil. Place water, cooking rack (or basket), and bowl in cooker. Close cover securely. Place pressure regulator on vent pipe. COOK 5 MINUTES at 15 pounds pressure. Let pressure drop of its own accord. Open pressure cooker and let rice steam, uncovered, 5 minutes. Stir in lemon rind.

● ● ● ● ● ● ●

Artichokes with Herbs and Sauce

Servings: 4
Per Serving
Calories: 307
Fat: 23.4 g
Sodium: 83 mg
Cholesterol: 193 mg

2 large or 4 medium artichokes	Salt
1 small carrot	Pepper
1 small onion	1 cup dry white wine
3 tablespoons olive oil	½ cup water
2 tablespoons chopped parsley	* * * * *
½ teaspoon dried basil	3 egg yolks
½ teaspoon dried oregano	½ cup whipping cream
½ teaspoon dillweed	1 tablespoon lemon juice
1 clove garlic	Pinch cayenne pepper

Cut 1½ inches off top of each artichoke. Cut off stems. Pull leaves open at top, remove center leaves and scrape out choke with grapefruit spoon. Combine carrot, onion, oil, parsley, dried herbs, garlic, salt, and pepper to taste in blender or food processor. Process until finely chopped. Stuff herb mixture between leaves of artichokes. Place cooking rack (or basket), wine, and water in 6- or 8-quart pressure cooker. Place artichokes on rack (or in basket). Close cover securely. Place pressure regulator on vent pipe. COOK 10 MINUTES at 15 pounds pressure. Quick cool cooker. Remove artichokes and rack (or basket). Keep warm. Boil liquid left in pressure cooker until reduced to ¾ cup. Beat egg yolks with cream. Whisk in small amount of the hot broth. Whisk egg mixture into remaining broth. Cook and stir over low heat until sauce thickens. Stir in lemon juice and cayenne pepper. Serve sauce with artichokes.

Intro

Basics

Appetizers

Soups
and
Stocks

Meats

Poultry

Seafood

Vegetables

Breads

Desserts

Whole
Meal
Magic

143

Vegetable Terrine

1 (10-ounce) package frozen spinach, thawed
1 teaspoon butter
2 eggs, beaten
2 tablespoons fresh bread crumbs
¼ teaspoon salt
⅛ teaspoon ground nutmeg
⅛ teaspoon pepper
1 (16-ounce) can stewed tomatoes
1 teaspoon butter
⅛ teaspoon garlic powder
⅛ teaspoon cayenne pepper

1 egg, beaten
2 tablespoons fresh bread crumbs
1½ cups sliced green onions
1 teaspoon butter
¼ cup whipping cream
¼ teaspoon salt
1 egg, beaten
2 tablespoons fresh bread crumbs
2 cups hot water

* * * * *

Yogurt Tomato Sauce (recipe follows)

❀ **Low Calorie**
Servings: 8
Per Serving
Calories: 118
Fat: 6.7 g
Sodium: 444 mg
Cholesterol: 119 mg

Drain spinach, pressing out excess moisture. Cook spinach with 1 teaspoon butter in saucepan over medium heat until all moisture is evaporated. Cool slightly. Stir in 2 eggs, 2 tablespoons bread crumbs, ¼ teaspoon salt, nutmeg, and pepper. Reserve. Drain tomatoes thoroughly. Reserve juice for sauce. Chop tomatoes slightly. Cook with 1 teaspoon butter, garlic powder, and cayenne pepper in saucepan over medium heat until all moisture is evaporated. Cool slightly. Stir in 1 egg and 2 tablespoons bread crumbs. Sauté onions in 1 teaspoon butter over medium heat until tender. Add cream and ¼ teaspoon salt. Cook until all cream is absorbed. Cool slightly. Stir in 1 egg and 2 tablespoons bread crumbs. To assemble: Butter 1-quart mold that fits loosely on rack (or in basket) in pressure cooker. Spread ½ cup of the spinach mixture in bottom of mold. Top with tomato mixture, then with onion mixture. Top with remaining spinach mixture. Cover mold securely with aluminum foil. Place cooking rack (or basket) and hot water in pressure cooker. Place mold on rack (or in basket). Close cover securely. Place pressure regulator on vent pipe. COOK 12 MINUTES at 15 pounds pressure. Quick cool cooker. Remove terrine and let cool in mold on wire rack 10 minutes. Unmold terrine. Refrigerate until chilled.

Yogurt Tomato Sauce

Reserved juice from stewed tomatoes
1 teaspoon sugar
1 teaspoon cornstarch
1 teaspoon cold water

1 teaspoon prepared horseradish
¼ teaspoon salt
½ cup yogurt

Boil juice reserved from stewed tomatoes until reduced to ½ cup. Mix sugar, cornstarch, cold water, horseradish, and salt. Stir into reduced juice. Cook and stir until sauce boils and thickens. Let cool. Stir in yogurt. Serve with Vegetable Terrine.

Pot Roast Royale...Page 79

Fruit and Beets...Page 128

Herbed Chicken with Potatoes...Page 103

Turkey Sausage with Potato Salad...Page 105

Date Nut Bread...Page 163

Braised Duckling Menu...Pages 182-183

146

Beet Borscht...Page 35

Parsnip Salad...Page 132

Turnip Timbales...Page 137

Curried Carrots...Page 131

Savory Swedes...Page 139

147

Mahogany-Sauced Lamb Shanks...Page 74

Caramel Custards...Page 172

Steamed Christmas Pudding...Page 175

150

Creole Cod...Page 118

San Francisco Chicken...Page 93

Almond Cod with Peas...Page 121

153

Garden Vegetable Salad...Page 132

Potato Salad...Page 125

Daube of Beef...Page 72

154

Fish Spin Wheels...Page 120

MINIMUM TIME
POTATOES 3
SEA FOOD 2
BROCCOLI 1
CARROTS 1
CHICKEN 5
RICE 5

PRESTO®
STAINLESS STEEL
PRESSURE COOKER

Chicken Couscous with Raspberry Vinegar…Page 101

Fruit Betty...Page 170

Pork Chops for Two...Page 77

Chicken Pot Pie...Page 104

Paprika and Pepper Short Ribs...Page 73

Orange Cheesecake with Orange Sauce...Page 173

159

Lentil Soup with Franks...Page 35

9 Breads

> **"**Moist, sweet, and often studded with dried fruits and nuts...**"**

If you think homemade bread only comes out of the oven, you're missing something truly wonderful—steamed breads. Moist, sweet, and often studded with dried fruits and nuts, steamed breads probably trace their roots back to the traditional steamed "puddings" that graced English tea tables and holiday groaning boards.

But in the new world, Yankee ingenuity soon found ways to incorporate common American ingredients into these breads for a unique taste treat. Boston Brown Bread, made with yellow cornmeal and molasses, soon captivated the colonists. Other creative versions followed, though none achieved the fame and following of this true American original.

The only serious drawback to preparing steamed breads was time. Most required prolonged and steady steaming in a kettle. But the introduction of the pressure cooker changed all that! Cooking times were reduced dramatically. The ordinary cooking time for *Steamed Brown Bread*, for example, was three hours compared to only one hour in the pressure cooker.

9

We've collected an assortment of all-American steamed bread recipes that were developed specifically for quick and easy preparation in the pressure cooker. Try them. After just one bite of *Apple-Walnut Whiskey Bread* or *Steamed Berry Bread*, you'll wonder why anyone would ever again bother baking dessert bread in an oven.

● ● ● ● ● ● ●

❀ *Low Calorie*
Servings: 12
Per Serving
Calories: 135
Fat: 5.3 g
Sodium: 130 mg
Cholesterol: 18 mg

Steamed Berry Bread

½ medium orange
¼ cup packed brown sugar
¼ cup walnut pieces
1 egg
2 tablespoons vegetable oil, optional

1 cup sliced strawberries or whole raspberries
1 (7½- or 8-ounce) package corn muffin mix
4 cups hot water

Remove orange part of orange rind in thin strips. Remove and discard white part of rind. Coarsely chop orange pulp. Process orange rind and half the brown sugar in food processor until finely chopped. Add nuts. Chop with on-and-off pulses. Transfer to bowl. Process remaining brown sugar, egg, and oil for a few seconds. Add orange pulp and berries. Process with on-and-off pulses until chopped. Pour half the fruit mixture over orange rind mixture in bowl. Top with half the muffin mix. Repeat layers with remaining fruit and muffin mix. Stir just until moistened. Spoon into greased 1-quart mold that fits loosely on rack (or in basket) in 6- or 8-quart pressure cooker. Cover bowl securely with aluminum foil. Place cooking rack (or basket) and water in pressure cooker. Place mold on rack (or in basket). Close cover securely. Do not place pressure regulator on vent pipe. COOK 10 MINUTES with steam flowing **very gently** through vent pipe. Place pressure regulator on vent pipe. COOK 35 MINUTES at 15 pounds pressure. Let pressure drop of its own accord. Remove bread and let cool in mold on wire rack 15 minutes. Remove bread from mold. Let cool on wire rack. Makes 1 loaf.

Date Nut Bread

1¼ cups all-purpose flour
½ cup coarsely chopped walnuts
⅓ cup sugar
1 tablespoon baking powder
¼ teaspoon salt
⅔ cup chopped dates
1 egg

⅔ cup water
¼ cup mayonnaise
1 teaspoon vanilla
4 cups hot water

* * * * *

Danish or other cream cheese

❁ *Low Calorie*
Servings: 12
Per Serving
Calories: 168
Fat: 7.2 g
Sodium: 159 mg
Cholesterol: 20 mg

(Shown on page 145)

Mix flour, walnuts, sugar, baking powder, and salt. Stir in dates. Beat egg, ⅔ cup water, mayonnaise, and vanilla until smooth. Add to flour mixture. Stir just until moistened. Pour into greased 1-quart casserole or soufflé dish that fits loosely on rack (or in basket) in 6- or 8-quart pressure cooker. Cover casserole securely with aluminum foil. Place cooking rack (or basket) and 4 cups water in pressure cooker. Place casserole on rack (or in basket). Close cover securely. Place pressure regulator on vent pipe. COOK 40 MINUTES at 15 pounds pressure. Let pressure drop of its own accord. Remove bread and let cool in casserole on wire rack. Remove bread from casserole. Refrigerate until chilled. Cut into thin slices. Serve with cheese. Makes 1 loaf.

● ● ● ● ● ● ●

Apple-Walnut Whiskey Bread

½ cup all-purpose flour
¼ cup whole wheat flour
¼ cup sugar
1 teaspoon baking powder
½ teaspoon baking soda
½ teaspoon salt
½ teaspoon ground cinnamon
¼ teaspoon ground allspice

2 eggs, beaten
¼ cup vegetable oil
¼ cup apple butter
½ cup chopped walnuts
⅓ cup chopped apples
1 tablespoon whiskey, optional
½ teaspoon vanilla
5 cups water

❁ *Low Calorie*
Servings: 12
Per Serving
Calories: 144
Fat: 8.5 g
Sodium: 161 mg
Cholesterol: 35 mg

Mix flours, sugar, baking powder, baking soda, salt, and spices. Stir in remaining ingredients except water. Pour into greased loaf pan, 6 x 2¼ x 2 inches. Cover pan securely with greased aluminum foil. Place cooking rack (or basket) and water in 6- or 8-quart pressure cooker. Place loaf pan on rack (or in basket). Close cover securely. Do not place pressure regulator on vent pipe. COOK 45 MINUTES with steam flowing **very gently** through vent pipe. Remove bread and let cool in loaf pan on wire rack 5 minutes. Remove bread from pan. Let cool on wire rack. Makes 1 loaf.

Intro

Basics

Appetizers

Soups and Stocks

Meats

Poultry

Seafood

Vegetables

Breads

Desserts

Whole Meal Magic

Pumpkin-Raisin Bread

½ cup packed light brown sugar
2 eggs, beaten
¼ cup vegetable oil
¼ cup canned solid-pack pumpkin
¾ cup all-purpose flour
1 teaspoon baking powder

½ teaspoon baking soda
1 teaspoon ground cinnamon
¼ teaspoon ground cardamom
¼ teaspoon salt
½ cup golden raisins
5 cups water

❋ Low Calorie
Servings: 12
Per Serving
Calories: 135
Fat: 5.5 g
Sodium: 120 mg
Cholesterol: 35 mg

Mix brown sugar, eggs, oil, and pumpkin. Mix flour, baking powder, baking soda, spices, and salt. Stir into egg mixture. Stir in raisins. Pour into greased loaf pan, 6 x 2¼ x 2 inches. Cover pan securely with greased aluminum foil. Place cooking rack (or basket) and water in 6- or 8-quart pressure cooker. Place loaf pan on rack (or in basket). Close cover securely. Do not place pressure regulator on vent pipe. COOK 45 MINUTES with steam flowing **very gently** through vent pipe. Remove bread and let cool in loaf pan on wire rack 5 minutes. Remove bread from pan. Let cool on wire rack. Makes 1 loaf.

● ● ● ● ● ● ●

Steamed Zucchini Bread

❋ Low Calorie
Servings: 12
Per Serving
Calories: 145
Fat: 6.5 g
Sodium: 123 mg
Cholesterol: 18 mg

(Shown on page 54)

1 egg
¼ cup packed brown sugar
2 tablespoons vegetable oil
1½ teaspoons ground cinnamon
1 cup shredded zucchini

1 (7½- or 8-ounce) package oatmeal or corn muffin mix
¼ cup dark raisins
¼ cup chopped walnuts
4 cups hot water

Beat egg, brown sugar, oil, and cinnamon. Add zucchini and muffin mix. Stir just until moistened. Stir in raisins and walnuts. Pour into greased 1-quart mold or metal bowl that fits loosely on rack (or in basket) in pressure cooker. Cover mold securely with aluminum foil. Place cooking rack (or basket) and hot water in pressure cooker. Place mold on rack (or in basket). Close cover securely. Place pressure regulator on vent pipe. COOK 40 MINUTES at 15 pounds pressure. Let pressure drop of its own accord. Remove bread and let cool in mold on wire rack 15 minutes. Remove bread from mold. Serve warm. Makes 1 loaf.

NOTE: *For smaller loaves of bread, use two greased 1-pound cans. COOK 30 MINUTES at 15 pounds pressure.*

Steamed Brown Bread

✳ *Low Calorie*
❤ *Low Cholesterol*
Servings: 8
Per Serving
Calories: 235
Fat: 6.3 g
Sodium: 466 mg
Cholesterol: 27 mg

1 cup cornmeal
¾ cup all-purpose flour
1 teaspoon baking powder
1 teaspoon baking soda
1 teaspoon salt
3 tablespoons vegetable shortening

½ cup chopped dates
¾ cup buttermilk
½ cup dark molasses
1 egg, beaten
5 cups hot water

Mix cornmeal, flour, baking powder, baking soda, and salt in bowl. Cut in shortening. Stir in dates. Add buttermilk, molasses, and egg. Stir just until moistened. Pour into greased 5-cup mold that fits loosely on rack (or in basket) in 6- or 8-quart pressure cooker. Cover mold securely with aluminum foil. Place cooking rack (or basket) and hot water in pressure cooker. Place mold on rack (or in basket). Close cover securely. Do not place pressure regulator on vent pipe. COOK 30 MINUTES with steam flowing **very gently** through vent pipe. Place pressure regulator on vent pipe. COOK 30 MINUTES at 15 pounds pressure. Quick cool cooker. Remove bread and let cool in mold on wire rack 5 minutes. Remove bread from mold. Let cool on wire rack. Makes 1 loaf.

Intro

Basics

Appetizers

Soups
and
Stocks

Meats

Poultry

Seafood

Vegetables

Breads

Desserts

Whole
Meal
Magic

Notes

10. Desserts

> **"So don't wait for a special occasion to try one of these sweet, soothing treats."**

For those who crave "comfort" foods with a touch of sweetness, desserts from the pressure cooker provide all the solace anyone could desire! The kinds of desserts that harken us back to homier times in our history are exactly what the pressure cooker does best.

It's perfect for the steamed Christmas puddings of early American celebrations. The frugal, yet satisfying, bread puddings of the thirties and forties. The towering cheesecakes that epitomized the easy, sweet life of the fifties. And all the silky custards, moist pudding cakes, and stewed fruit compotes consumed whenever and wherever the opportunity arose.

Like all foods, desserts cooked in the pressure cooker offer faster—almost instant—gratification. Pressure cooking makes it possible to indulge in an old-fashioned rice pudding or fruit "betty" even when time is at a minimum. So don't wait for a special occasion to try one of these sweet, soothing treats.

10

Nut-Crusted Chocolate Cheesecake

2 tablespoons margarine, softened
¼ cup vanilla wafer crumbs
2 tablespoons finely ground walnuts
2 tablespoons finely ground pecans
1 (8-ounce) package cream cheese, softened

½ cup granulated sugar
¼ cup packed light brown sugar
2 eggs
¼ cup unsweetened cocoa
1 tablespoon all-purpose flour
3 cups water

❋ *Low Calorie*
Servings: 10
Per Serving
Calories: 200
Fat: 12.2 g
Sodium: 119 mg
Cholesterol: 70 mg

Line 1-quart soufflé dish that fits loosely on rack (or in basket) in 6- or 8-quart pressure cooker with aluminum foil; coat with margarine. Mix wafer crumbs and nuts and press on bottom and halfway up side of dish. Beat cream cheese until fluffy in small bowl. Beat in sugars. Beat in eggs. Mix in cocoa and flour. Pour into soufflé dish. Cover dish securely with aluminum foil. Place cooking rack (or basket) and water in pressure cooker. Place soufflé dish on rack (or in basket). Close cover securely. Place pressure regulator on vent pipe. COOK 40 MINUTES at 15 pounds pressure. Let pressure drop of its own accord. Remove cheesecake and let cool in dish on wire rack. Refrigerate 8 hours or overnight. Remove cheesecake from dish by lifting foil. Carefully remove foil.

● ● ● ● ● ● ●

❋ *Low Calorie*
Servings: 8
Per Serving
Calories: 222
Fat: 14.8 g
Sodium: 139 mg
Cholesterol: 38 mg

Creamiest Rice Pudding

2 cups hot milk
1 cup whipping cream or half-and-half
6 tablespoons margarine, melted
¾ cup long grain rice
⅔ cup granulated sugar

1 teaspoon ground cinnamon
1 tablespoon grated lemon rind
2½ cups water
* * * * *
Light brown sugar

Mix milk, cream, margarine, rice, sugar, cinnamon, and lemon rind in metal bowl that fits loosely on rack (or in basket) in 6- or 8-quart pressure cooker. Cover bowl securely with aluminum foil. Place cooking rack (or basket), water, and bowl in cooker. Close cover securely. Place pressure regulator on vent pipe. COOK 25 MINUTES at 15 pounds pressure. Let pressure drop of its own accord. Open pressure cooker and let rice steam, uncovered, 15 minutes. Stir to mix. Spoon into bowls; sprinkle lightly with brown sugar.

Apple Whole Wheat Bread Pudding ✾ ❤

Low Calorie
Low Cholesterol
Servings: 6
Per Serving
Calories: 194
Fat: 3.7 g
Sodium: 328 mg
Cholesterol: 75 mg

4 cups cubed stale whole
   wheat bread
⅓ cup golden raisins
1¼ cups milk
½ cup apple butter
2 eggs, beaten
2 tablespoons sugar
1 teaspoon vanilla

½ teaspoon salt
½ teaspoon ground cinnamon
¼ teaspoon ground nutmeg
3 cups water

* * * * *

Vanilla ice cream or frozen
yogurt

Combine bread and raisins. Mix remaining ingredients except water and ice cream. Pour over bread mixture. Toss and let stand 20 minutes. Spoon into greased 1-quart soufflé dish that fits loosely on rack (or in basket) in 6- or 8-quart pressure cooker. Cover dish securely with greased aluminum foil. Place cooking rack (or basket) and water in pressure cooker. Place soufflé dish on rack (or in basket). Close cover securely. Place pressure regulator on vent pipe. COOK 25 MINUTES at 15 pounds pressure. Quick cool cooker. Serve warm with ice cream.

● ● ● ● ● ● ●

Petite Pumpkin Custards

✾ Low Calorie
Servings: 8
Per Serving
Calories: 207
Fat: 6.3 g
Sodium: 89 mg
Cholesterol: 97 mg

(Shown on page 57)

1 (16-ounce) can solid-pack
   pumpkin
1 (14-ounce) can sweetened
   condensed milk
3 eggs, beaten
1 teaspoon ground cinnamon

1 teaspoon finely chopped
   candied ginger, optional
¼ teaspoon ground cloves
2 cups hot water

* * * * *

Whipped cream, optional

Mix pumpkin, milk, eggs, cinnamon, ginger, and cloves. Pour into eight 6-ounce custard cups. Cover each cup securely with aluminum foil. Place cooking rack (or basket) and hot water in pressure cooker. Place single layer of custard cups on rack (or in basket). Close cover securely. Place pressure regulator on vent pipe. COOK 10 MINUTES at 15 pounds pressure. Quick cool cooker. Remove custards. Repeat above procedure to cook remaining custards. Refrigerate until chilled. Serve with whipped cream.

Intro

Basics

Appetizers

Soups
and
Stocks

Meats

Poultry

Seafood

Vegetables

Breads

Desserts

Whole
Meal
Magic

169

Fruit Betty

1 cup coconut bar cookie crumbs (16 cookies)
1 tablespoon butter or margarine, melted

2 tablespoons orange juice
1 peach, apple, or small pear, pared and sliced
2 cups water

Servings: 2
Per Serving
Calories: 599
Fat: 26 g
Sodium: 438 mg
Cholesterol: 15 mg

(Shown on page 158)

Combine coconut bar cookie crumbs, butter, and orange juice. Arrange 2 slices of peach in two 6-ounce custard cups. Layer crumbs and peaches in each cup. Cover each cup securely with aluminum foil. Place cooking rack (or basket) and water in pressure cooker. Place custard cups on cooking rack (or in basket). Close cover securely. Place pressure regulator on vent pipe. COOK 15 MINUTES at 15 pounds pressure. Quick cool cooker.

✿ *Low Calorie*
Servings: 10
Per Serving
Calories: 284
Fat: 17.7 g
Sodium: 141 mg
Cholesterol: 80 mg

Cannoli Cheesecake

2 tablespoons margarine, softened
½ cup vanilla wafer crumbs
1 teaspoon ground cinnamon
1 (8-ounce) package cream cheese, softened
¼ cup ricotta cheese
½ cup granulated sugar
½ cup powdered sugar
2 eggs
1 tablespoon all-purpose flour
¾ teaspoon vanilla

½ teaspoon ground cinnamon
¼ cup mini semisweet chocolate pieces
¼ cup chopped pecans
2 tablespoons finely chopped glacé fruit and peel
3 cups water
* * * * *
½ cup sour cream or sour half-and-half
Ground cinnamon

Line 1-quart soufflé dish that fits loosely on rack (or in basket) in 6- or 8-quart pressure cooker with aluminum foil; coat with margarine. Mix wafer crumbs and 1 teaspoon cinnamon and press on bottom and halfway up side of dish. Beat cream cheese until fluffy in small bowl. Beat in ricotta cheese and sugars. Beat in eggs. Mix in flour, vanilla, and ½ teaspoon cinnamon. Stir in chocolate pieces, pecans, and glacé fruit. Pour into soufflé dish. Cover dish securely with aluminum foil. Place cooking rack (or basket) and water in pressure cooker. Place soufflé dish on rack (or in basket). Close cover securely. Place pressure regulator on vent pipe. COOK 40 MINUTES at 15 pounds pressure. Let pressure drop of its own accord. Remove cheesecake and let cool in dish on wire rack. Refrigerate 8 hours or overnight. Remove cheesecake from dish by lifting foil. Carefully remove foil. Spread sour cream on top of cheesecake. Sprinkle lightly with cinnamon.

Coconut Custards

2 eggs, beaten
2 tablespoons sugar
¼ teaspoon salt
1 teaspoon rum extract

1½ cups milk
¼ cup shredded coconut
1½ cups hot water

Mix eggs, sugar, salt, and rum extract. Add milk and mix well. Place 1 tablespoon coconut in each of four 5-ounce custard cups that fit loosely on rack (or in basket) in 6- or 8-quart pressure cooker. Pour custard into cups. Cover each cup securely with aluminum foil. Place cooking rack (or basket) and hot water in pressure cooker. Place custard cups on rack (or in basket). Close cover securely. Place pressure regulator on vent pipe. COOK 3 MINUTES at 15 pounds pressure. Quick cool cooker. Remove custard cups to cool on wire rack. Refrigerate until chilled.

● ● ● ● ● ●

Steamed Chocolate Pudding Cake

⅔ cup granulated sugar
3 tablespoons margarine, softened
1 egg, beaten
½ cup buttermilk
½ teaspoon vanilla
¾ cup all-purpose flour

¼ cup unsweetened cocoa
2 teaspoons baking powder
½ teaspoon baking soda
¼ teaspoon salt
5 cups water

＊ ＊ ＊ ＊ ＊
Powdered sugar

Mix granulated sugar and margarine. Stir in egg, buttermilk, and vanilla. Mix flour, cocoa, baking powder, baking soda, and salt. Stir into egg mixture. Pour into greased 1-quart bowl or soufflé dish that fits loosely on rack (or in basket) in 6- or 8-quart pressure cooker. Cover bowl securely with greased aluminum foil. Place cooking rack (or basket) and water in pressure cooker. Place bowl on rack (or in basket). Close cover securely. Do not place pressure regulator on vent pipe. COOK 60 MINUTES with steam flowing **very gently** through vent pipe. Remove cake and let cool in bowl on wire rack 5 minutes. Remove from bowl. Let cool on wire rack. Sprinkle with powdered sugar before serving.

Intro

Basics

Appetizers

Soups
and
Stocks

Meats

Poultry

Seafood

Vegetables

Breads

Desserts

Whole
Meal
Magic

10

Ruby Pears

4 large pears, pared
1 (26-ounce) bottle Beaujolais wine or grape juice
1 (12-ounce) jar red currant jelly
1 lemon

2 sprigs fresh rosemary
½ vanilla bean
4 whole cloves
4 whole peppercorns

❤ **Low Cholesterol**

Servings: 4
Per Serving
Calories: 465
Fat: 0.7 g
Sodium: 23 mg
Cholesterol: 0

(Shown on page 55)

Core pears from the bottom, keeping top and stem intact. Combine wine and jelly in 6- or 8-quart pressure cooker. Heat and stir to melt jelly. Pare thin strips of rind and squeeze juice from lemon. Add rind and juice to pressure cooker. Cut four 12-inch squares of aluminum foil. Dip a pear in jelly mixture and place on foil square. Bring four corners of foil up around pear and twist securely at top to seal. Repeat to wrap all pears. Add remaining ingredients to pressure cooker. Place cooking rack (or basket) in pressure cooker. Place pears upright on rack (or in basket). Close cover securely. Place pressure regulator on vent pipe. COOK 4 TO 8 MINUTES* at 15 pounds pressure. Quick cool cooker. Carefully remove pears from foil and place in deep bowl. Pour hot wine mixture over pears. Let cool; then refrigerate for at least 24 hours.

*Bosc pears take longer to cook. Check doneness before removing pears. If necessary, close cooker and cook a few minutes longer.

● ● ● ● ● ●

❀ **Low Calorie**

Servings: 4
Per Serving
Calories: 173
Fat: 4.3 g
Sodium: 77 mg
Cholesterol: 113 mg

(Shown on page 149)

Caramel Custards

1½ cups milk
1 cinnamon stick
¼ cup sugar
¼ cup hot water

2 eggs, beaten
¼ cup sugar
Pinch salt
1½ cups hot water

Heat milk with cinnamon stick over low heat just to boiling point. Cool slightly. Caramelize ¼ cup sugar in small heavy skillet over medium heat. Carefully add ¼ cup hot water and stir until caramel dissolves. Divide caramelized sugar among four 5-ounce custard cups that fit loosely on rack (or in basket) in 6- or 8-quart pressure cooker. Discard cinnamon stick from milk. Whisk small amount of hot milk into eggs. Gradually whisk egg mixture into remaining hot milk. Stir in ¼ cup sugar and salt until dissolved. Pour over caramel in custard cups. Cover each cup securely with aluminum foil. Place cooking rack (or basket) and 1½ cups hot water in pressure cooker. Place custard cups on rack (or in basket). Close cover securely. Place pressure regulator on vent pipe. COOK 5 MINUTES at 15 pounds pressure. Quick cool cooker. Remove custard cups to cool on wire rack. Refrigerate until chilled. Unmold before serving.

Orange Cheesecake with Orange Sauce

1 (11-ounce) can mandarin oranges, well drained, juice reserved
1 (8-ounce) package cream cheese
1 (3-ounce) package cream cheese
½ cup sugar

2 eggs
½ cup toasted whole wheat bread crumbs
2½ cups water

* * * * *

¼ cup sugar
2 teaspoons cornstarch
½ teaspoon orange extract

❋ Low Calorie
Servings: 10
Per Serving
Calories: 199
Fat: 12.1 g
Sodium: 119 mg
Cholesterol: 77 mg

(Shown on page 159)

Line soufflé dish or 6-inch spring form pan that fits loosely on rack (or in basket) in 6- or 8-quart pressure cooker with aluminum foil. Decoratively arrange orange sections in bottom of dish. Beat cream cheese until smooth. Beat in ½ cup sugar. Beat in eggs, one at a time. Pour mixture over orange sections. Sprinkle with crumbs. Cover dish securely with aluminum foil. Place cooking rack (or basket) and water in pressure cooker. Place dish on rack (or in basket). Close cover securely. Place pressure regulator on vent pipe. COOK 20 MINUTES at 15 pounds pressure. Quick cool cooker. Remove cheesecake and cool in soufflé dish on wire rack. Loosen edges and unmold. Refrigerate until chilled. Meanwhile, mix ¼ cup sugar and cornstarch in small saucepan. Stir in ½ cup reserved mandarin orange juice. Cook and stir until sauce boils and thickens. Stir in extract. Let cool. Spoon sauce over cheesecake.

● ● ● ● ● ● ●

Lemony Bread Pudding

3 slices raisin bread
1 tablespoon butter or margarine, softened
2 tablespoons sugar
⅛ teaspoon nutmeg

½ teaspoon lemon extract
2 eggs, slightly beaten
2 cups milk, scalded
2 cups water

❋ Low Calorie
Servings: 6
Per Serving
Calories: 132
Fat: 5.6 g
Sodium: 128 mg
Cholesterol: 82 mg

Spread bread with butter or margarine and cut into cubes. Place in buttered bowl that fits loosely on rack (or in basket) in 6- or 8-quart pressure cooker. Combine sugar, nutmeg, lemon extract, and eggs. Slowly add hot milk to egg mixture, stirring to mix. Pour mixture over bread cubes. Cover bowl securely with aluminum foil. Place cooking rack (or basket), water, and bowl in pressure cooker. Close cover securely. Place pressure regulator on vent pipe. COOK 10 MINUTES at 15 pounds pressure. Quick cool cooker. Remove bowl and spoon out individual servings. Serve with fresh berries, if desired.

Intro

Basics

Appetizers

Soups and Stocks

Meats

Poultry

Seafood

Vegetables

Breads

Desserts

Whole Meal Magic

173

10. Pecan Carrot Cake

1 cup shredded carrots	½ teaspoon baking soda
½ cup vegetable oil	1 teaspoon ground cinnamon
2 eggs, beaten	½ teaspoon ground nutmeg
⅓ cup granulated sugar	¼ teaspoon ground allspice
⅓ cup packed light brown sugar	¼ teaspoon salt
1 teaspoon vanilla	5 cups water
¾ cup all-purpose flour	* * * * *
⅓ cup chopped pecans	1 tablespoon margarine, softened
2 tablespoons quick-cooking oats	½ cup powdered sugar
1 teaspoon baking powder	Milk

Servings: 8
Per Serving
Calories: 324
Fat: 18.9 g
Sodium: 199 mg
Cholesterol: 53 mg

Mix carrots, oil, eggs, granulated sugar, brown sugar, and vanilla. Mix flour, pecans, oats, baking powder, baking soda, spices, and salt. Stir into egg mixture. Pour into greased 1-quart glass bowl or soufflé dish that fits loosely on rack (or in basket) in pressure cooker. Cover bowl securely with greased aluminum foil. Place cooking rack (or basket) and water in pressure cooker. Place bowl on rack (or in basket). Close cover securely. Do not place pressure regulator on vent pipe. COOK 60 MINUTES with steam flowing **very gently** through vent pipe. Remove cake and let cool in bowl on wire rack 5 minutes. Remove cake from bowl. Let cool on wire rack. Mix margarine, powdered sugar, and enough milk to make glaze consistency. Drizzle over cake.

✻ *Low Calorie*
Servings: 4
Per Serving
Calories: 224
Fat: 7.8 g
Sodium: 33 mg
Cholesterol: 8 mg

(Shown on page 50)

Stuffed Apples

¼ cup golden raisins	½ teaspoon ground cinnamon
½ cup dry red wine	4 cooking apples
¼ cup chopped nuts	1 tablespoon butter
2 tablespoons sugar	1½ cups water
½ teaspoon grated orange rind	

Soak raisins in wine for at least 30 minutes. Drain, reserving wine. Combine raisins, nuts, sugar, orange rind, and cinnamon. Core apples, cutting to but not through bottoms. Pare top one-third of apples. Place each apple on square of aluminum foil that is large enough to completely wrap apple. Fill centers with raisin mixture. Top each with one-fourth of the butter. Wrap foil around apple, pinching firmly together at top. Place cooking rack (or basket), reserved wine, and water in pressure cooker. Place apples on rack (or in basket). Close cover securely. Place pressure regulator on vent pipe. COOK 10 MINUTES at 15 pounds pressure. Quick cool cooker.

Steamed Christmas Pudding

¼ cup bourbon or apple juice
1½ cups finely chopped glacé cherries
¼ cup currants or dark raisins
¼ cup coarsely chopped walnuts
¼ cup coarsely chopped pecans
1½ cups fresh white bread crumbs
⅓ cup all-purpose flour
¾ teaspoon ground cinnamon

½ teaspoon ground allspice
¼ teaspoon ground nutmeg
½ teaspoon salt
½ cup margarine, softened
½ cup packed light brown sugar
½ cup granulated sugar
2 eggs, beaten
5 cups water

* * * * *

Whipped cream

❋ *Low Calorie*
Servings: 12
Per Serving
Calories: 216
Fat: 8.2 g
Sodium: 219 mg
Cholesterol: 36 mg

(Shown on page 150)

Pour bourbon over fruits and nuts. Let stand 1 hour. Mix bread crumbs, flour, spices, and salt. Beat margarine, sugars, and eggs. Mix in bread crumb mixture. Stir in fruit and nut mixture. Pack into greased 1-quart soufflé dish that fits loosely on rack (or in basket) in 6- or 8-quart pressure cooker. Cover dish securely with aluminum foil. Place cooking rack (or basket) and water in pressure cooker. Place soufflé dish on rack (or in basket). Close cover securely. Do not place pressure regulator on vent pipe. COOK 20 MINUTES with steam flowing **very gently** through vent pipe. Place pressure regulator on vent pipe. COOK 25 MINUTES at 15 pounds pressure. Let pressure drop of its own accord. Remove cake and let cool in soufflé dish on wire rack. Serve with whipped cream.

● ● ● ● ● ● ●

Pear Mold

1 small orange
1 cup cornflake crumbs
¼ cup sugar
¼ cup butter, softened
½ teaspoon ground cinnamon
3 medium pears or apples, pared, thinly sliced

3 cups water

* * * * *

Whipping cream or vanilla ice cream

❋ *Low Calorie*
Servings: 6
Per Serving
Calories: 200
Fat: 8 g
Sodium: 193 mg
Cholesterol: 20 mg

Grate rind and squeeze juice from orange. Mix rind and juice with cornflake crumbs, sugar, butter, and cinnamon. Place one-third of the pears in buttered bowl that fits loosely on rack (or in basket) in 6- or 8-quart pressure cooker. Top with one-third of the crumb mixture. Repeat layers two more times. Cover bowl securely with aluminum foil. Place cooking rack (or basket) and water in pressure cooker. Place bowl on rack (or in basket). Close cover securely. Place pressure regulator on vent pipe. COOK 15 MINUTES at 15 pounds pressure. Quick cool cooker. Remove pear mold and cool on wire rack. Serve with cream.

Intro

Basics

Appetizers

Soups and Stocks

Meats

Poultry

Seafood

Vegetables

Breads

Desserts

Whole Meal Magic

175

10. Steamed Banana Pudding with Plum Sauce

¼ cup butter or margarine	¼ teaspoon baking soda
⅔ cup sugar	¼ teaspoon ground nutmeg
2 eggs	⅛ teaspoon ground cloves
¾ cup mashed banana (1 large)	¾ cup grated carrot
1 teaspoon vanilla	½ cup chopped pecans
1½ cups all-purpose flour	5 cups hot water
2 teaspoons baking powder	* * * * *
½ teaspoon ground cinnamon	Plum Sauce (recipe follows)
¼ teaspoon salt	

❤ *Low Cholesterol*

Servings: 8
Per Serving
Calories: 381
Fat: 11.9 g
Sodium: 324 mg
Cholesterol: 69 mg

Cream butter and sugar. Beat in eggs, one at a time. Stir in banana and vanilla. Sift flour, baking powder, cinnamon, salt, baking soda, nutmeg, and cloves together. Add to banana mixture. Stir in grated carrot and pecans. Spoon into well-buttered 1-quart mold that fits loosely on rack (or in basket) in 6- or 8-quart pressure cooker. Cover mold securely with aluminum foil. Place cooking rack (or basket) and hot water in pressure cooker. Place mold on rack (or in basket). Close cover securely. Do not place pressure regulator on vent pipe. COOK 30 MINUTES with steam flowing **very gently** through vent pipe. Place pressure regulator on vent pipe. COOK 40 MINUTES at 15 pounds pressure. Quick cool cooker. Remove pudding and let cool in mold on wire rack. Top with Plum Sauce.

Plum Sauce

¼ cup lemon juice	½ pound fresh plums, cut into
½ cup firmly packed light	eighths (3-4 medium) or ½
brown sugar	can (1 pound, 14 ounces)
¼ cup honey	whole, unpeeled purple
1 teaspoon minced candied	plums with ⅓ cup syrup
ginger	1 tablespoon cornstarch
¼ teaspoon salt	2 tablespoons water

In small saucepan, combine lemon juice, brown sugar, honey, ginger, salt, and plums. Heat to boiling while stirring occasionally. Reduce heat. Simmer and cook 20 to 30 minutes or until plums are soft. Blend together cornstarch and water. Stir into plum mixture. Heat to boiling while stirring constantly. Boil 2 minutes or until thickened. Makes about 1½ cups sauce. Serve warm over pudding.

Bread & Butter Pudding with Raspberry Sauce

Servings: 6
Per Serving
Calories: 352
Fat: 9.1 g
Sodium: 267 mg
Cholesterol: 123 mg

Intro

Basics

Appetizers

Soups
and
Stocks

Meats

Poultry

Seafood

Vegetables

Breads

Desserts

Whole
Meal
Magic

2 tablespoons butter, softened
5 slices French bread, ½ inch
   thick
   Ground nutmeg
2 eggs
1 egg yolk
⅓ cup sugar
½ teaspoon vanilla
2 cups milk, heated
4 cups water
   Raspberry Sauce (recipe
   follows)

Butter one side of bread slices. Sprinkle lightly with nutmeg. Cut into quarters. Arrange in 1-quart buttered casserole that fits loosely on rack (or in basket) in 6- or 8-quart pressure cooker. Beat eggs, egg yolk, sugar, and vanilla. Slowly add milk to egg mixture. Pour over bread. Cover casserole securely with aluminum foil. Place cooking rack (or basket) and water in pressure cooker. Place casserole on rack (or in basket). Close cover securely. Do not place pressure regulator on vent pipe. COOK 5 MINUTES with steam flowing **very gently** through vent pipe. Place pressure regulator on vent pipe. COOK 10 MINUTES at 15 pounds pressure. Quick cool cooker. Serve warm or at room temperature with Raspberry Sauce.

Raspberry Sauce

1 (10-ounce) package frozen
   raspberries, thawed
½ cup red currant jelly
1 tablespoon cornstarch

Combine raspberries, jelly, and cornstarch in saucepan. Cook and stir until sauce boils and thickens. Strain sauce. Let cool.

Notes

11. Whole Meal Magic

"Simple, step-by-step instructions take you through the entire meal..."

E ver since the early days of cooking over an open fire, we have looked for ways to conserve both time and energy during meal preparation.

When World War II created fuel shortages, oven meals were seen as the answer. For these carefully choreographed meals, the entrée, vegetable, and dessert all baked in the same oven, at the same temperature, at the same time.

Convenience foods were the cure during the fifties and sixties. Homemakers saved steps by creating complete meals using a combination of food products that had some or all of the preparation already done. It could be a sauce made from canned condensed soup, dumplings from a packaged biscuit mix, or frozen, breaded, and precooked fish fillets that simply needed reheating.

Today a common solution to this universal problem is supplementing one or two homemade dishes with prepared foods from the supermarket deli or restaurant take-out counter.

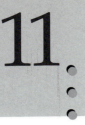

11.

There is another answer, however, that allows plenty of time and energy conservation without any compromises. It's pressure cooking, of course!

One of the handiest advantages of the versatile pressure cooker is its ability to prepare several foods at one time, in only one pot, without an unwanted intermingling of flavors. By using the cooking rack or basket to keep certain foods out of the cooking liquid, each food—whether it's a main dish, side dish, or dessert— retains its own individual character.

The following menus and recipes demonstrate the "whole meal magic" of pressure cooking. Simple, step-by-step instructions take you through the entire meal preparation process from start to speedy finish. You'll find menus to fit almost any occasion or situation—from hurried weekday suppers to special dinner parties or celebrations. Try one next time you're searching for a solution to the time and energy crunch.

● ● ● ● ● ● ●

Beef Taco Menu

Guacamole Dip with Chips

*Beef and Bean Tacos

Sliced Avocados and Tomatoes with Cilantro

*Banana Flan

Margaritas, Beer, or Cinnamon Coffee

(Serves 4 people)

*Recipes included

Beef and Bean Tacos

1 pound boneless beef round steak (½ inch thick)
1 tablespoon vegetable oil
  Garlic salt
  Pepper
¾ cup medium or mild chunky salsa
¾ cup orange juice
½ cup water

* * * * *

1 (15-ounce) can refried beans
2 tablespoons yellow cornmeal
2 tablespoons water
8 flour tortillas or taco shells
  Toppings: Shredded lettuce, chopped tomato, chopped onion, shredded Monterey Jack cheese, sour cream, salsa

♥ *Low Cholesterol*
Servings: 4
Per Serving
Calories: 547
Fat: 14.7 g
Sodium: 671 mg
Cholesterol: 72 mg

● ● ● ● ● ● ●

Banana Flan

1¼ cups milk
1 egg, beaten
4 teaspoons sugar
½ teaspoon vanilla

½ small banana

* * * * *

¼ teaspoon ground cinnamon

✿ *Low Calorie*
♥ *Low Cholesterol*
Servings: 4
Per Serving
Calories: 86
Fat: 2.8 g
Sodium: 54 mg
Cholesterol: 59 mg

How to Prepare

1. Beef and Bean Tacos: Cut steak across grain into strips 2 inches long and ¼ inch wide. Heat oil in 6- or 8-quart pressure cooker over medium heat. Sauté beef until browned. Season to taste with garlic salt and pepper. Stir in salsa, orange juice, and ½ cup water. Place cooking rack (or basket) on top of meat.

2. Banana Flan: Heat milk to simmering in small saucepan. Remove from heat. Mix egg, sugar, and vanilla; whisk into milk. Thinly slice banana into four individual custard cups. Pour milk mixture into custard cups. Cover cups securely with aluminum foil. Place cups on rack (or in basket) in pressure cooker.

3. Pressure Cook: Close cover securely. Place pressure regulator on vent pipe. COOK 5 MINUTES at 15 pounds pressure. Quick cool cooker. Remove custard cups. Remove foil. Sprinkle custards with cinnamon. Cool on wire rack. Remove meat mixture and cooking rack (or basket), reserving cooking liquid in pressure cooker. Stir beans into cooking liquid. Mix cornmeal and 2 tablespoons water. Stir into bean mixture. Cook over medium-high heat until thickened.

4. To Complete: Spread bean mixture on tortillas. Spoon meat mixture on beans. Spoon desired toppings on meat and roll up.

Intro

Basics

Appetizers

Soups and Stocks

Meats

Poultry

Seafood

Vegetables

Breads

Desserts

Whole Meal Magic

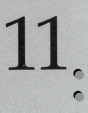

Braised Duckling Menu

*Beer-Braised Duckling

*Apple-Caraway Sauerkraut

*Dilled Potatoes

Greens and Sliced Beets with Vinaigrette Dressing

German Chocolate Cake

Beer, Coffee, or Tea

(Serves 4 people)

*Recipes included

Apple-Caraway Sauerkraut

❀ *Low Calorie*
❤ *Low Cholesterol*

Servings: 4
Per Serving
Calories: 141
Fat: 4 g
Sodium: 1502 mg
Cholesterol: 0

(Shown on page 146)

1 tablespoon vegetable oil	¼ cup dry white wine or apple juice
½ cup chopped onion	1 large tart apple, pared, cored, cut into ½-inch wedges
½ teaspoon caraway seeds, crushed	✳ ✳ ✳ ✳ ✳
1 teaspoon all-purpose flour	¼ cup dark raisins
2 (16-ounce) cans sauerkraut, rinsed, drained	

Beer-Braised Duckling

1 tablespoon vegetable oil
4 pound duckling, cut into quarters
1 (12-ounce) can beer

1 cup water

* * * * *

Minced parsley

Servings: 4
Per Serving
Calories: 729
Fat: 59.2 g
Sodium: 121 mg
Cholesterol: 165 mg

(Shown on page 146)

● ● ● ● ● ● ●

Dilled Potatoes

4 medium red-skinned potatoes, unpared, cut into quarters

* * * * *

1 tablespoon margarine
¼ teaspoon dillweed
Salt
Pepper

✿ *Low Calorie*
♥ *Low Cholesterol*
Servings: 4
Per Serving
Calories: 85
Fat: 1.5 g
Sodium: 36 mg
Cholesterol: 0

(Shown on page 146)

How to Prepare:

1. Apple-Caraway Sauerkraut: Heat oil in 6- or 8-quart pressure cooker over medium heat. Sauté onion and caraway seeds until onion is tender. Stir in flour. Cook 1 minute. Stir in sauerkraut and wine. Spoon mixture into shallow foil packet. Top with apple wedges. Seal packet.

2. Beer-Braised Duckling: Heat oil in pressure cooker over medium heat. Brown duck on all sides. Discard excess fat. Add beer and water to pressure cooker.

3. Pressure Cook: Close cover securely. Place pressure regulator on vent pipe. COOK 12 MINUTES at 15 pounds pressure. Let pressure drop of its own accord. Place cooking rack (or basket) on top of duck. Place sauerkraut packet and potatoes on rack (or in basket). Close cover securely. Place pressure regulator on vent pipe. COOK 5 MINUTES at 15 pounds pressure. Quick cool cooker.

4. To Complete: Season potatoes with margarine, dillweed, salt, and pepper. Stir raisins into sauerkraut. Remove duck to platter. Sprinkle with parsley. Skim fat from cooking juices. Serve juices with duck, if desired.

Intro

Basics

Appetizers

Soups and Stocks

Meats

Poultry

Seafood

Vegetables

Breads

Desserts

Whole Meal Magic

11.

Cubed Steak Menu

Cornbread-Stuffed Cubed Steaks

Turnip-Apple Purée

Fresh Green Beans

Head Lettuce Wedges with Ranch Dressing

Angel Food Cake with Sherbet

Coffee, Tea, or Milk

(Serves 4 people)

*Recipes included

Cornbread-Stuffed Cubed Steaks

Servings: 4
Per Serving
Calories: 442
Fat: 17.4 g
Sodium: 1146 mg
Cholesterol: 131 mg

2 cups cornbread stuffing mix
¼ cup finely chopped onion
¼ cup finely chopped green pepper
1 teaspoon very finely chopped jalapeño chile
1 egg, beaten
½ cup warm beef stock or broth
2 tablespoons margarine, melted
4 beef cubed steaks (about 1 pound)

1 tablespoon vegetable oil
Salt
Pepper
1 cup beef stock or broth
½ cup water
* * * * *
⅓ cup chopped tomatoes
2 teaspoons cornstarch
2 tablespoons cold water
Dash red pepper sauce

Turnip-Apple Purée

2 small tart cooking apples,
  pared, cored, cut into quarters
2 medium turnips, pared, cut
  into quarters (12 ounces)
  * * * * *
¼ cup whipping cream or half-
  and-half, heated

½-1 teaspoon prepared
  horseradish
½ teaspoon crushed caraway
  seeds
Salt
White pepper

❀ Low Calorie
Servings: 4
Per Serving
Calories: 100
Fat: 5 g
Sodium: 53 mg
Cholesterol: 16 mg

● ● ● ● ● ● ●

Fresh Green Beans

1 pound fresh green beans
  * * * * *
1 tablespoon margarine

Salt
Pepper

❀ Low Calorie
♥ Low Cholesterol
Servings: 4
Per Serving
Calories: 51
Fat: 1.7 g
Sodium: 36 mg
Cholesterol: 0

How to Prepare:

1. Cornbread-Stuffed Cubed Steaks: Combine stuffing mix, onion, green pepper, and chile. Add egg, ½ cup beef stock, and margarine. Toss to moisten evenly. Divide stuffing on top of steaks. Fold sides of steaks together. Fasten with wooden picks. Heat oil in 6- or 8-quart pressure cooker over medium heat. Brown steaks. Sprinkle with salt and pepper. Add 1 cup beef stock and ½ cup water to pressure cooker. Place cooking rack (or basket) on top of steaks.

2. Turnip-Apple Purée: Place apple quarters into two shallow foil packets. Seal packets. Place turnips and apple packets on one side of rack (or basket).

3. Pressure Cook: Close cover securely. Place pressure regulator on vent pipe. COOK 4 MINUTES at 15 pounds pressure. Quick cool cooker.

4. Fresh Green Beans: Place green beans on rack (or in basket).

5. Pressure Cook: Close cover securely. Place pressure regulator on vent pipe. COOK 1 TO 2 MINUTES at 15 pounds pressure. Quick cool cooker. Remove steaks, vegetables, apples, and rack (or basket). Keep warm. Add tomatoes to stock remaining in pressure cooker. Heat to boiling. Mix cornstarch with 2 table-spoons cold water. Stir into stock mixture. Cook and stir until sauce boils and thickens. Season to taste with pepper sauce, salt, and pepper.

6. To Complete: Arrange steaks on serving plate; top with tomato sauce. Mash turnips and apples with whipping cream, horseradish, and caraway seeds; season with salt and pepper. Season green beans with margarine, salt, and pepper.

Intro

Basics

Appetizers

Soups
and
Stocks

Meats

Poultry

Seafood

Vegetables

Breads

Desserts

Whole
Meal
Magic

11

Stroganoff Menu

Three-Meat Stroganoff

Peas with Sliced Mushrooms

Sliced Tomato Salad with Basil

Gingered Pears

Coffee, Tea, or Milk

(Serves 4 people)

Recipes included

● ● ● ● ● ● ●

✿ *Low Calorie*
Servings: 4
Per Serving
Calories: 300
Fat: 14 g
Sodium: 409 mg
Cholesterol: 112 mg

Three-Meat Stroganoff

2 tablespoons olive or
vegetable oil
8 ounces lean boneless beef,
cut into ¾-inch cubes
8 ounces lean boneless veal,
cut into ¾-inch cubes
8 ounces lean boneless pork,
cut into ¾-inch cubes
1 cup sliced onion
1 tablespoon paprika

¼ teaspoon dried marjoram
1½ cups beef stock or broth
1 tablespoon red wine vinegar
* * * * *
1 tablespoon tomato paste
½ cup sour cream or sour half-
and-half, optional
Salt
Pepper
Cooked egg noodles

Peas with Sliced Mushrooms

2 cups frozen peas
½ cup drained canned sliced
   mushrooms

     * * * * *

1 tablespoon margarine
  Salt
  Pepper

✿ *Low Calorie*
♥ *Low Cholesterol*
Servings: 4
Per Serving
Calories: 77
Fat: 1.7 g
Sodium: 102 mg
Cholesterol: 0

● ● ● ● ● ● ●

Gingered Pears

2 medium pears, cored, cut
  into halves

     * * * * *

¾ cup dry sherry or apple juice
⅓ cup sugar

1 tablespoon finely chopped
  crystalized ginger
1 small cinnamon stick
2 tablespoons chopped walnuts
  Whipped cream

✿ *Low Calorie*
♥ *Low Cholesterol*
Servings: 4
Per Serving
Calories: 192
Fat: 2.5 g
Sodium: 2 mg
Cholesterol: 0

How to Prepare:

1. Three-Meat Stroganoff: Heat oil in 6- or 8-quart pressure cooker over medium heat. Brown meats on all sides and remove. Add onion to pressure cooker. Sauté until tender. Stir in paprika, marjoram, beef stock, vinegar, and meats.

2. Peas with Sliced Mushrooms: Combine peas and mushrooms. Wrap in 1 or 2 aluminum foil packets.

3. Pressure Cook: Close cover securely. Place pressure regulator on vent pipe. COOK 10 MINUTES at 15 pounds pressure. Let pressure drop of its own accord. Place cooking rack (or basket) on top of meat mixture. Place packets of peas on rack (or in basket). Arrange pears, cut sides up, on rack (or in basket). Close cover securely. Place pressure regulator on vent pipe. COOK 2 MINUTES at 15 pounds pressure. Quick cool cooker.

4. To Complete: Heat sherry, sugar, ginger, and cinnamon stick to boiling in small saucepan. Simmer rapidly until mixture thickens to a thin syrup consistency, about 8 minutes. Let stand until serving time. Season peas with margarine, salt, and pepper. Stir tomato paste and sour cream into stroganoff; season with salt and pepper. Serve stroganoff over noodles. Discard cinnamon stick from syrup. Stir in walnuts. Spoon over pears in shallow bowls. Top with whipped cream.

Intro

Basics

Appetizers

Soups
and
Stocks

Meats

Poultry

Seafood

Vegetables

Breads

Desserts

Whole
Meal
Magic

187

Pork Chop Menu

Blackened Pork Chops

Pecan Broccoli

Parslied Rice

Assorted Fruit Salad with Honey Dressing

Marmalade Apples

Coffee, Tea, or Milk

(Serves 2 people)

*Recipes included

✿ *Low Calorie*
Servings: 2
Per Serving
Calories: 259
Fat: 20.8 g
Sodium: 312 mg
Cholesterol: 59 mg

Blackened Pork Chops

2 **boneless pork chops (about 8 ounces)**	½ **teaspoon garlic powder**
2 **teaspoons vegetable oil**	¼ **teaspoon dried basil**
½ **teaspoon dried oregano**	¼ **teaspoon salt**
½ **teaspoon ground cumin**	⅛ **teaspoon filé powder, optional**
½ **teaspoon paprika**	1 **tablespoon vegetable oil**
½ **teaspoon cayenne pepper**	1½ **cups water**

Pecan Broccoli

8 ounces broccoli

* * * * *

2 teaspoons margarine
   Salt

Pepper
2 tablespoons chopped toasted
   pecans

❋ Low Calorie
Servings: 2
Per Serving
Calories: 93
Fat: 6.9 g
Sodium: 74 mg
Cholesterol: 0

● ● ● ● ● ●

Marmalade Apples

2 tart cooking apples
2 tablespoons margarine,
   softened
2 tablespoons packed brown
   sugar

2 tablespoons bitter orange
   marmalade
2 tablespoons toasted slivered
   almonds

❋ Low Calorie
Servings: 2
Per Serving
Calories: 275
Fat: 9.9 g
Sodium: 139 mg
Cholesterol: 0

How to Prepare:

1. Blackened Pork Chops: Rub pork chops with 2 teaspoons oil. Combine herbs, salt, and filé powder. Rub into chops. Let stand 5 minutes. Heat 1 tablespoon oil in 6- or 8-quart pressure cooker over medium heat. Brown chops on both sides and remove. Place greased cooking rack (or basket) and 1½ cups water in pressure cooker. Place chops on rack (or in basket).

2. Pecan Broccoli: Separate broccoli flowerettes. Cut stalks into ¾-inch pieces. Wrap broccoli in aluminum foil packet.

3. Marmalade Apples: Core apples, cutting to but not through the bottoms. Mix margarine and brown sugar. Spoon about 1 tablespoon mixture into center of each apple. Top with marmalade, almonds, and remaining margarine mixture, dividing evenly.

4. Pressure Cook: Close cover securely. Place pressure regulator on vent pipe. COOK 3 MINUTES at 15 pounds pressure. Quick cool cooker. Arrange broccoli packet and apples on rack (or in basket) with pork chops. Close cover securely. Place pressure regulator on vent pipe. COOK 3 MINUTES at 15 pounds pressure. Quick cool cooker.

5. To Complete: Arrange pork chops on serving plate. Season broccoli with margarine, salt, and pepper; sprinkle with pecans. Place apples in shallow dishes.

Intro

Basics

Appetizers

Soups
and
Stocks

Meats

Poultry

Seafood

Vegetables

Breads

Desserts

Whole
Meal
Magic

11

Stuffed Trout Menu

Stuffed Rainbow Trout

Spaghetti Squash Parmesan

Baby Carrots and Pearl Onions

Spinach Salad with Poppy Seed Dressing

Lemon Meringue Pie

Wine, Coffee, or Tea

(Serves 4 people)

*Recipes included

❦ Low Calorie
Servings: 4
Per Serving
Calories: 210
Fat: 9.2 g
Sodium: 357 mg
Cholesterol: 65 mg

Stuffed Rainbow Trout

1 tablespoon margarine
¼ cup slivered almonds
¼ cup chopped onion
¼ cup thinly sliced celery
½ teaspoon dried tarragon
⅛ teaspoon dillweed
½ cup dry unseasoned bread cubes
½ teaspoon grated lemon rind

½ teaspoon salt
⅛ teaspoon pepper
2-3 tablespoons dry white wine or chicken stock or broth
2 rainbow trout, dressed (about 8 ounces each)

* * * * *

Lemon wedges
Parsley sprigs

Spaghetti Squash Parmesan

1½ cups water
½ spaghetti squash, seeds discarded (about 1 pound)

* * * * *

2 teaspoons margarine

1-2 tablespoons grated Parmesan cheese
Salt
Pepper

❋ *Low Calorie*
Servings: 4
Per Serving
Calories: 30
Fat: 1.5 g
Sodium: 53 mg
Cholesterol: 1 mg

● ● ● ● ● ● ●

Baby Carrots and Pearl Onions

12 ounces baby carrots, pared
½ (10-ounce) package frozen pearl onions

* * * * *

1 tablespoon margarine

1 tablespoon packed light brown sugar
Salt
Pepper

❋ *Low Calorie*
♥ *Low Cholesterol*
Servings: 4
Per Serving
Calories: 72
Fat: 1.6 g
Sodium: 68 mg
Cholesterol: 0

How to Prepare:

1. Stuffed Rainbow Trout: Heat margarine in 6- or 8-quart pressure cooker over medium heat. Cook almonds until toasted. Remove almonds. Add onion, celery, tarragon, and dillweed to pressure cooker. Sauté until onion is tender. Combine onion mixture, almonds, bread cubes, lemon rind, salt, and pepper in medium bowl. Toss with enough wine to moisten. Cut heads off fish, if necessary, to fit in pressure cooker. Fill cavities of fish with stuffing. Secure with skewers or wooden picks. Cut a piece of aluminum foil that will fit across bottom and up sides of pressure cooker. Fold foil lengthwise in half.

2. Spaghetti Squash Parmesan: Place 1½ cups water and squash, cut side up, in pressure cooker. Place cooking rack (or basket) on squash.

3. Baby Carrots and Pearl Onions: Combine carrots and onions in 1 or 2 aluminum foil packets. Place foil strip for fish on cooking rack (or in basket). Place fish on foil. Place vegetable packets on rack (or in basket).

4. Pressure Cook: Close cover securely. Place pressure regulator on vent pipe. COOK 4 MINUTES at 15 pounds pressure. Quick cool cooker. Remove fish and vegetable packets. If squash is not tender, close pressure cooker cover securely. Place pressure regulator on vent pipe and COOK 1 TO 2 MINUTES longer. Quick cool cooker.

5. To Complete: Arrange fish on serving plate; garnish with lemon wedges and parsley. Transfer carrots and onions to serving bowl; season with margarine, brown sugar, salt, and pepper. Fluff strands of spaghetti squash with fork; mix with margarine. Sprinkle with cheese; season with salt and pepper.

Intro

Basics

Appetizers

Soups and Stocks

Meats

Poultry

Seafood

Vegetables

Breads

Desserts

Whole Meal Magic

191

Chicken Breast Menu

*Chicken Breasts Supreme

*Herbed Potatoes

*Honey Glazed Carrots

Hot Dinner Rolls

Strawberry Compote

Milk, Coffee, or Tea

(Serves 4 people)

*Recipes Included

❀ *Low Calorie*
❤ *Low Cholesterol*

Servings: 4
Per Serving
Calories: 209
Fat: 7 g
Sodium: 356 mg
Cholesterol: 73 mg

Chicken Breasts Supreme

1 tablespoon vegetable oil	2 tablespoons chopped onion
2 chicken breasts, skinned, cut in half, lengthwise	1 teaspoon paprika
	Salt
1½ cups chicken broth	Pepper
½ cup white wine	

Herbed Potatoes

4 small potatoes, pared, cut into ¾-inch thick slices

* * * * *

1 tablespoon margarine

2 teaspoons parsley
½ teaspoon oregano
¼ teaspoon garlic salt

❀ *Low Calorie*
♥ *Low Cholesterol*
Servings: 4
Per Serving
Calories: 131
Fat: 1.6 g
Sodium: 128 mg
Cholesterol: 0

● ● ● ● ● ● ●

Honey Glazed Carrots

6 carrots, peeled, cut diagonally into 1-inch pieces

* * * * *

2 tablespoons margarine, melted
1 teaspoon honey

❀ *Low Calorie*
Servings: 4
Per Serving
Calories: 77
Fat: 3.1 g
Sodium: 103 mg
Cholesterol: 0

How to Prepare:

1. Chicken Breasts Supreme: Heat oil in 6- or 8-quart pressure cooker over medium heat. Brown chicken on all sides. Mix chicken broth, wine, onion, paprika, salt, and pepper. Pour over chicken.

2. Pressure Cook: Close cover securely. Place pressure regulator on vent pipe. COOK 2 MINUTES at 15 pounds pressure. Quick cool cooker.

3. Herbed Potatoes and Honey Glazed Carrots: Place potatoes and carrots on rack (or in basket).

4. Pressure Cook: Close cover securely. Place pressure regulator on vent pipe. COOK 5 MINUTES at 15 pounds pressure. Quick cool cooker. Meanwhile, heat together margarine and honey. Keep warm. Remove carrots, potatoes, and chicken. Cook and stir until remaining liquid from pressure cooker boils and thickens. Keep warm.

5. To Complete: Season potatoes with margarine, parsley, oregano, and garlic salt. Season carrots with margarine and honey mixture. Serve sauce over chicken.

Intro

Basics

Appetizers

Soups
and
Stocks

Meats

Poultry

Seafood

Vegetables

Breads

Desserts

Whole
Meal
Magic

193

11.

Swedish Meatball Menu

Swedish Meatballs

Golden Whipped Taters

Rye Bread

Date Coconut Custard

Milk, Coffee, or Tea

(Serves 4 people)

Recipes included

Date Coconut Custard

❋ Low Calorie
Servings: 4
Per Serving
Calories: 187
Fat: 6 g
Sodium: 160 mg
Cholesterol: 113 mg

2	eggs, beaten	1½	cups milk
2	tablespoons sugar	8	dates, pitted, chopped
⅛	teaspoon salt	4	tablespoons shredded coconut
1	tablespoon vanilla	¼	teaspoon nutmeg

Swedish Meatballs

½ pound lean ground beef
½ pound ground pork
2 eggs
2 tablespoons parsley
1 tablespoon flour
1 clove garlic, minced
⅛ teaspoon paprika

⅛ teaspoon nutmeg
⅛ teaspoon ginger
 Salt
 Pepper
2 tablespoons vegetable oil
1½ cups water

❋ *Low Calorie*
Servings: 4
Per Serving
Calories: 286
Fat: 18.3 g
Sodium: 91 mg
Cholesterol: 182 mg

● ● ● ● ● ● ●

Golden Whipped Taters

6 cups cubed (¾-inch) rutabaga
2 cups cubed (¾-inch) potatoes
2 cups water
2 tablespoons minced onion

1 cup shredded Cheddar cheese
1 tablespoon sugar
1 tablespoon minced parsley
1 teaspoon salt
¼ teaspoon pepper

❋ *Low Calorie*
Servings: 4
Per Serving
Calories: 286
Fat: 10 g
Sodium: 759 mg
Cholesterol: 30 mg

* * * * *

How to Prepare:

1. Date Coconut Custard: Combine egg, sugar, salt, and vanilla. Add milk; mix well. Divide chopped dates and coconut equally into four 5-ounce custard cups that fit loosely on rack (or in basket) in 6- or 8-quart pressure cooker. Pour custard mixture into each cup. Sprinkle nutmeg on top. Cover each cup securely with aluminum foil. Set aside.

2. Swedish Meatballs: Combine all ingredients except oil and water; mold into medium-sized meatballs. Heat oil in pressure cooker over medium heat. Brown meatballs. Add 1½ cups water.

3. Pressure Cook: Place cooking rack (or basket) over meatballs. Arrange custard cups on rack (or in basket). Close cover securely. Place pressure regulator on vent pipe. COOK 5 MINUTES at 15 pounds pressure. Quick cool cooker. Remove custards and set aside. Remove meatballs and keep warm. Thicken liquid for gravy, if desired. Set aside and keep warm.

4. Golden Whipped Taters: Combine rutabaga, potatoes, 2 cups water, and onion in pressure cooker. Close cover securely. Place pressure regulator on vent pipe. COOK 3 MINUTES at 15 pounds pressure. Let pressure drop of its own accord. Drain vegetables. Whip until smooth. Stir in cheese, sugar, parsley, salt, and pepper.

5. To Complete: Serve warm Taters with meatballs and gravy.

Intro

Basics

Appetizers

Soups
and
Stocks

Meats

Poultry

Seafood

Vegetables

Breads

Desserts

Whole
Meal
Magic

195

Thanksgiving Dinner

*Hunter's Turkey

*Broccoli with Lemon 'n Butter

Cranberry Relish

Harvest Corn Muffins

*Pumpkin Custards

Wine, Coffee, or Tea

(Serves 2 people)

* Recipes Included

- - - - - - -

Hunter's Turkey

Servings: 2
Per Serving
Calories: 303
Fat: 14 g
Sodium: 860 mg
Cholesterol: 83 mg

1 tablespoon vegetable oil	½ bay leaf
1 pound turkey thigh	¼ teaspoon thyme
1 cup chicken broth	¼ teaspoon marjoram
1 cup water	¼ teaspoon Worcestershire
1 tablespoon chopped onion	sauce
½ cup tomato sauce	

Broccoli with Lemon 'n Butter

8 ounces broccoli
1 tablespoon margarine, melted

4 thin lemon slices

❀ Low Calorie
Servings: 2
Per Serving
Calories: 82
Fat: 6.1 g
Sodium: 95 mg
Cholesterol: 0

● ● ● ● ● ● ●

Pumpkin Custards

½ cup milk
1 egg, beaten
¾ cup cooked mashed pumpkin
⅛ teaspoon salt
¼ cup packed brown sugar

2 teaspoons sugar
½ teaspoon ground cinnamon
⅛ teaspoon ground ginger
⅛ teaspoon ground cloves

* * * * *

Whipped cream, optional

❀ Low Calorie
Servings: 2
Per Serving
Calories: 204
Fat: 3.7 g
Sodium: 204 mg
Cholesterol: 111 mg

How to Prepare:

1. Hunter's Turkey: Heat oil in 6- or 8-quart pressure cooker over medium heat. Brown turkey. Mix chicken broth, water, onion, tomato sauce, bay leaf, thyme, marjoram, and Worcestershire sauce. Pour over turkey. Place cooking rack (or basket) on top of meat.

2. Broccoli with Lemon 'n Butter: Separate broccoli flowerettes. Cut stalks into ¾-inch pieces. Place broccoli into shallow foil packets. Dot with margarine. Arrange lemon slices on top. Seal foil packets.

3. Pumpkin Custards: Combine milk, egg, pumpkin, salt, brown sugar, sugar, cinnamon, ginger, and cloves. Pour into two 6-ounce custard cups. Cover cups securely with aluminum foil. Place custard cups on rack (or in basket) in pressure cooker.

4. Pressure Cook: Close cover securely. Place pressure regulator on vent pipe. COOK 10 MINUTES at 15 pounds pressure. Quick cool cooker. Remove custard cups and chill. Place broccoli packet on rack (or in basket). Close cover securely. Place pressure regulator on vent pipe. COOK 5 MINUTES at 15 pounds pressure. Quick cool cooker.

5. To Complete: Arrange turkey on serving plate. Transfer broccoli to serving bowl. Top pumpkin custard with whipped cream, if desired.

Intro

Basics

Appetizers

Soups
and
Stocks

Meats

Poultry

Seafood

Vegetables

Breads

Desserts

Whole
Meal
Magic

Lamb Kabobs Menu

Lamb Kabobs

Brown Rice

Spinach with Feta Cheese Dressing

Baklava

Beer, Coffee, or Tea

(Serves 4 people)

*Recipes included

Lamb Kabobs

✻ *Low Calorie*
Servings: 4
Per Serving
Calories: 242
Fat: 8.6 g
Sodium: 48 mg
Cholesterol: 57 mg

1 tablespoon vegetable oil
1 pound lean boneless lamb, cut into 1-inch cubes
  Salt
  Pepper
1 onion, cut into 8 chunks

1 green pepper, cut into 1-inch pieces
8 prunes, pitted
½ cup white wine
1 cup water

Brown Rice

1 cup natural brown rice   2½ cups water
1½ cups water

● ● ● ● ● ● ●

✿ *Low Calorie*
❤ *Low Cholesterol*
Servings: 4
Per Serving
Calories: 171
Fat: 1.3 g
Sodium: 3 mg
Cholesterol: 0

How to Prepare:

1. Lamb Kabobs: Heat oil in 6- or 8-quart pressure cooker over medium heat. Brown lamb cubes on all sides. Season to taste with salt and pepper. Place lamb on 4 skewers alternately with onion, green pepper, and prunes.

2. Brown Rice: Combine brown rice and 1½ cups water in metal bowl that fits loosely on rack (or in basket) in 6- or 8-quart pressure cooker. Cover bowl securely with aluminum foil. Place 2½ cups water, cooking rack (or basket), and metal bowl in cooker.

3. Pressure Cook: Close cover securely. Place pressure regulator on vent pipe. COOK 10 MINUTES at 15 pounds pressure. Let pressure drop of its own accord. Open cooker and let rice steam, uncovered, 5 minutes. Remove bowl and discard liquid from cooker. Place lamb kabobs on rack (or in basket). Add ½ cup white wine and 1 cup water. Place pressure regulator on vent pipe. COOK 1 MINUTE at 15 pounds pressure. Quick cool cooker.

4: To Complete: Arrange lamb kabobs over brown rice.

Intro

Basics

Appetizers

Soups
and
Stocks

Meats

Poultry

Seafood

Vegetables

Breads

Desserts

Whole
Meal
Magic

Notes